HOW TO PLAY
Better
GOLF

HOW TO PLAY
Better
GOLF

WARD LOCK

A WARD LOCK BOOK
First Published in the UK in 1991
by Ward Lock
Wellington House
125 Strand
London
WC2R 0BB
A Cassell Imprint
©Ward Lock Limited 1991
Reprinted 1993 (twice), 1995, 1996

Editor: Heather Thomas
Art Director: Rolando Ugolini
Illustrations: Rolando Ugolini

Designed and produced by SP Creative Design,
St Andrews House, 33 St Andrews Street South,
Bury St Edmunds, Suffolk

Text set in Stone Serif by Halcyon Type & Design Ltd, Ipswich
Printed and bound in Singapore

British Library Cataloguing in Publication Data

Authors, various
  How to play better golf
  1. Golf. Techniques
  I. Title
  796.3523
  ISBN 0-7063-6995-5

Contents

Contributors

A team of distinguished and experienced golf professionals have written this book. They are:

Nigel Blenkarne is the Club Professional at Parkstone Golf Club, Dorset, England. He competed for three years on the European Tour and has won several Pro-Am tournaments. He has co-written and presented an instructional video on Golf for Women.

Jim Christine is Golf Professional at Worplesdon Golf Club, Surrey, England. He is a Senior Swing Tutor with the PGA, and a regular contributor to *Golf World* magazine and a member of *Golf World's* teaching panel.

Craig DeFoy is the Golf Professional at Combe Hill Golf Club, Surrey, England. He was a tournament player on the European circuit for many years and represented Wales seven times in the World Cup. He is now the Welsh National Coach.

Pip Elson played on the European Tour for several years. He was Henry Cotton Rookie of the Year in 1973 and has twice been a runner-up in the Nigerian Open (in 1976 and 1979). He is now attached to Mentmore Golf Club and continues to play in Pro-Ams and company golf days.

Lawrence Farmer is the Golf Professional at West Middlesex Golf Club, England. He is an ex-European Tour player, and still plays regularly in Pro-Ams. He coaches the Middlesex County teams and Ricky Willison, the Great Britain amateur international.

Lee Fickling is the Golf Professional at Enfield Golf Club, Hertfordshire, England. He played on the European Tour, competes regularly in Pro-Ams, and specializes in repairing equipment.

Robin Mann is Director of Golf at Finn Valley Golf Centre, Ipswich, England. He played on the European Tour for several years and was 1985 UK Club Professional Champion. He has won the Double Suffolk Professional Championships seven times.

Tony Moore is the Head Golf Professional at St Mellion Golf Club, Cornwall, England. He coaches the county teams of both Devon and Cornwall and has taught several well-known golfers including Roger Winchester and Jonathan Langlead, the English Amateur Champion.

Chapter One

Equipment

Lee Fickling

EQUIPMENT

As golf professionals we are constantly asked by a wide variety of golfers: ' What golf equipment would suit me best?' This question is asked by novices who want to start up in golf as well as by more established players who want to purchase some new equipment to help improve their game. The most important items of equipment that concern all players, whether novices or low-handicappers, are the clubs – their suitability and price.

The next question to answer is: "Where do I go?" Of course, being a golf professional, I would suggest a PGA Approved Professional Shop. But why? At one of these shops you will get expert advice on equipment, help with your game and, later on, a comprehensive repair service, all from qualified experienced golf professionals rather than from shop assistants, some of whom may not even know how to play the game.

The staff in many High Street shops are also more likely to be concerned with their company's turnover and therefore may not be particularly interested in the individual requirements of their customers. In some cases, all they need do is make a sale without worrying a great deal about the suitability of the goods sold. However, a professional will make sure that his customers will be able to use the clubs he sells because he will be in constant contact with them through lessons and membership of a club.

The most important thing for the novice is to acquire the knowledge and technique he needs to enable him to play golf to the best of his ability. This can be achieved only through the services of a qualified golf professional. However, professionals are only human and most feel that their pupils should purchase their equipment at their pro shops rather than at a retail sports shop as they have everything in stock that a golfer, novice or otherwise, requires.

Opposite: Every golfer can benefit from having the right equipment, and the clubs that suit his or her game, height and build. The shaft length, swingweight, grip size and even the loft of the clubs can affect your swing. In a competition, you are permitted to carry a maximum of 14 clubs.

Clubs for novices

Starting with the novice, the best suggestion is either to buy a second-hand set of clubs in good condition or a quality starter set. At this stage it is not good policy to overspend. If you are starting out in golf, you may not know yet whether it is going to be your game. If indeed it does prove to be so, then you still do not know what standard you will eventually reach – another good reason for not overspending at this stage.

A good professional will always be prepared to take his customer to the practice range to assess his current needs and advise on the best equipment for him. Being able to recommend the most suitable equipment for the individual does not always mean the most expensive. For the novice, many reputable companies offer their lower-end models as loss leaders. This means that quality is usually very high as they sell their products with the aim of attracting their customers to purchase their top-price models at a later date when they feel that they have improved.

The price of many top-range clubs is determined to a large extent by the amount of marketing carried out, not simply because of the higher quality materials used. The degree of workmanship that goes into producing these clubs, involving more precision and careful balance, especially in the shafts and grips, contributes to the higher quality. However, these factors will benefit only the more experienced golfer. Once the novice has become a more competent player he will probably wish to take advantage of these superior clubs, and he can trade in his second-hand or starter set and buy a set of clubs that will improve his play and complement his game.

Clubs for more experienced golfers

Once you have mastered the basic skills and techniques, you can consult the professional on purchasing a better set of clubs. You will find that you have now moved into the widest market in golf. By now, you will have some idea of what you require to help your individual game. You can discuss with the professional which of the models you prefer, with particular reference to the shape of the club, and ask him to make recommendations. This will involve deciding between a game-improving club, i.e. heel and toe weighted or peripheral weighted, and a blade-type club.

Game-improvement clubs: these are designed for middle-handicap golfers and cater for off-centre shots, by enlarging the sweet spot of the clubface and therefore allowing for a margin of error.

The two main types mentioned are easily explained. A heel and toe weighted club has the weight distributed at both ends of the clubhead, thereby widening the sweet spot. A peripheral weighted club has the weight evenly distributed around the perimeter of the clubhead, enlarging the sweet spot over all.

Blade clubs are the original shape of golf clubs with no thought given to helping the improving golfer. The weight on these clubs, generally, is evenly distributed, thereby leaving less room for error.

Regardless of whether you choose a game-improvement or a blade club, the professional will now be able to help recommend a suitable shaft flex, lie of the club, swing weight and thickness of grip.

With all these things in mind, you now have to decide how much you want to invest.

HOW TO PLAY BETTER GOLF

Swingweights

These vary on a scale from C0 to D9. The C1-C9 swingweights are generally for ladies as these are lighter than the D0-D9 range which are heavier and more suitable for men. Few clubs are made by manufacturers over D4 as the need becomes too heavy for even the best players to accelerate. On this basis, you might think that the lighter the swingweight, the faster you can make the club accelerate, but once you go below the C swingweights, it is impossible to 'feel' the clubhead and therefore control it.

Below are a few guidelines to choosing the right swinghead to suit you and your game:

C0-C5 Weaker lady player
C5-C8 Good lady player to older man
D0 Average man player
D2 Good man player

However, you should remember that as you become more proficient at golf, you will develop your own preferences for swingweights.

It is also important to get the right loft on your club, and the lofts table shows you the generally recognised lofts in degrees for irons and woods. Once again, as you become more experienced and skilled in the game, you will find that you prefer a particular loft which suits your personal play.

The shaft also is affected by the relevant swingweight and you must find the best one for you.

It is very important to attain the right balance between swingweight and shaft flex when choosing your clubs, and all these factors will be taken into consideration by the clubs fitter.

Opposite: Traditional-style 'blade' clubs (A) are preferred by most golf professionals. Generally, they are not suitable for beginners and high- to middle-handicap golfers, as they leave less room for error and demand a high degree of accuracy of strike unlike a peripherally weighted club (B) which has an enlarged sweet spot.

Lofts table (in degrees)

Woods	Tournament	Men	Ladies
No 1	10°	12°	12°
No 2	12°	14°	14°
No 3	14°	16°	16°
No 4	19°	20°	20°
No 5	23°	24°	25°

Lofts table (in degrees)

Irons	Tournament	Men	Ladies
No 2	18	19	–
No 3	22	23	24
No 4	26	27	28
No 5	30	31	32
No 6	34	35	36
No 7	38	39	40
No 8	42	43	44
No 9	46½	47	48
Pitching wedge	52	52	52
Sand iron	58	58	58

Anatomy of the golf club

The following basic terms describe the different parts of a golf club:

Clubface The total area of the clubhead where the ball should be struck.
Sweet spot The part of the clubface at which when the ball is struck correctly, the best shot is produced.
Hosel The part of the clubhead where the shaft enters the head.
Shank or heel The part of the clubhead nearest the hosel.
Toe The part of the clubface furthest from the hosel.
Sole The underneath of the clubhead which rests on the ground.

Utility clubs

Most players who have been playing golf over a period of time will have a full set of clubs, generally consisting of three woods, nine irons and a putter. However, with so many utility clubs available, players are now varying the clubs they carry as per the suggestions below:

1 and 2 irons These are used by golfers who struggle with woods, or by better players who prefer to use a long iron rather than a fairway wood to achieve greater accuracy.

7 woods These are used by ladies and older men who may not have the strength to accelerate the long irons and can make an easier swing with woods to achieve the same result.

Special wedges These can vary from 49° loft to 65° loft. Your choice will depend on the type of shot you are playing, i.e. if you struggle to loft the ball in the air, you may choose a very lofted wedge to help you, of perhaps 60°.

Customization

Many companies now offer custom-fit services, at no extra premium, on their top-of-the-range models. This means that a player can have a set of clubs tailored for his or her own physical size and golfing ability. Beginners cannot take advantage of this service because their ability

Below: Many low-handicap players prefer to use 1 and 2 irons rather than woods as they give them a higher degree of accuracy.
Opposite: The type of wedge that you choose will be governed by the shot that you are playing and also by the degree of loft demanded.

cannot be assessed accurately at that stage, but the more experienced golfer can benefit.

There are two types of customization:

1 By an experienced club fitter.

2 By computer.

Firstly, let us consider customization by an experienced club fitter. This entails going along to a company's workshop where the fitter will assess your height, build, size of hands and grip.

He will then watch you swing a club to assess your striking power. From these observations he will offer you several clubs with different specifications, one of which he will recommend as being right for you.

Secondly let us look at customization at a computer centre. In these workshops, the principle is essentially the same, but computers analyse the customer, rather than expert fitters. The advantage of the first option over the second is that the fitter judges all the different aspects of the customer, but the computer can only assess your swing at the given moment of impact. In my own experience, most golfers seem to be more satisfied with the judgement of a fitter rather than that given by a computer print-out. Also, the more reputable companies will offer you the option of making adjustments at a later date if necessary.

The final item in a set of clubs and one of the most important is a putter. Putters come in all shapes and sizes. Again, the price will be determined not only by the quality of the materials, but also by the precision of manufacture, as good balance is essential.

There are three main types – centre shaft, blade, and mallet head. Shafts are usually approximately the same length, with the exception of a modern innovation – a chin-height one as used by Sam Torrance. Your choice is a very personal matter, and most golfers accumulate a selection during their golfing lives.

Above: The new chin-height, long-shafted putter is favoured by Sam Torrance. Its exponents claim that it gives them more control and a greater degree of accuracy when putting.

Golf bags and trollies

Until now we have spoken only about clubs. There are still several other items of equipment that the novice will require. For instance, you will need a golf bag. You can purchase a cheap one in any sports shop, but you will find the best-quality ones in a good professional's shop.

Golf bags vary from very small weekender bags which carry only a few clubs up to a large professional-type one, carrying a full set plus every imaginable accessory. The materials used to make these bags range from PVC to nylon and, in rare cases, leather. All these factors plus the size of the bag contribute to its price.

If you decide on a large bag, you will also need a trolley. The quality of these again vary a great deal, but the larger the bag the stronger the trolley that you will need. The combination of bag and trolley is quite a heavy load but many companies overcome this problem by using light-weight alloys in the construction of their products. Electric trollies have come into their own recently – helping older players in particular to enjoy their golf by removing the effort required to pull a loaded trolley.

Golf shoes

Next we come to shoes, possibly the most important items apart from the clubs, as comfort is all important. As a novice, you should purchase shoes that will serve you all the year round. Possibly, the ideal pair is a breathable waterproof type with studs. Price is not really a major factor as the man-made materials used in this type cost far less than leather. As you progress, you will probably choose a leather pair for dry weather and keep your waterproof pair for wet conditions.

Many companies also produce spikeless shoes for lightness in warmer weather. As with golf bags, shoes can also be made in a variety of materials from cheap plastic to expensive skins. It is worth investing in good-quality ones, as comfort is the primary factor. A pair of well-fitting comfortable shoes that will last a long time may cost a lot of money, but they will probably be a better investment than a cheap pair which will soon wear out.

Waterproof suits

Possibly the last essential, especially in the UK, is a waterproof suit. Quality determines price once again. A nylon suit costs very little but does not really give enough protection as it is only showerproof. However, a Gore-tex suit offers total protection from the elements. Unfortunately using proven materials means high costs, and you may have to pay a very high price for one of these. Between these two extremes many other grades are available with varying degrees of comfort, protection and fabrics.

Chapter Two

The Set Up

Robin Mann

THE SET UP

The set up is 50 per cent of every golf shot that you will ever hit; and it is most important that you think of each shot as having two halves: the set up and the swing.

Have you ever been at the golf range or on the first tee when it is crowded and felt that everybody is watching you, and then thought, 'I had better get this one out of the way quickly'? Having decided that any set up will do, you give the ball a hit and then immediately regret it! On the first tee, the problem does not end there, as you have to hit another ball from the same place or, as some people do, walk down the fairway and then hit another ball. This can be an especially heartbreaking start to a round of golf, destroying all your confidence, and all because you did not take sufficient time to prepare the correct set up.

I am going to give you three main objectives that you will be trying to achieve:
1 Good 'thought patterns' to produce a repetitive and consistent set up.
2 A naturally athletic and relaxed position in the finished set up, thereby creating freedom of movement.
3 Trying to create the perfect impact in the set up.

In trying to produce a good set up, you can break it down into its four constituent parts. In fact, 'four' is now going to be one of your 'thought patterns'. The *four* main points are as follows:
1 The clubface.
2 The grip.
3 The stance and ball position.
4 Your posture.

Each of these *four* main sections has *four* points in each part and this makes it easy to remember. Also, if you lose the routine, sometimes a loose shot from others and a call of 'Fore' (different spelling) is a good way of helping you to remember your routine.

The better your set-up routine the better the player you will become. It will also help you to improve the quality of your 'bad' shots. Too many players are happy when they hit 10 good shots in 100 balls at the range, or make three pars on the golf course and lose six balls with the bad shots (that's 12 penalty shots!).

However, it is better not to hit any really good shots but instead to hit all the 'missed shots' in to play. It is the greatest feeling in golf when you don't hit the ball very well but you still manage to make a good score, yet it is very upsetting to hit a lot of good shots and still end up with a bad score.

Try watching better players than yourself, and observe the discipline in their set ups. The world's best top professionals have the best set ups and that is one of the reasons why they are the best; they hit the best 'bad' shots. They are closest to perfect impact in the set up and that is why it is easy for them to return and pass through perfect impact. Good players are forever checking their set-up routines, not just when they are going to hit a shot, but also between shots to constantly improve and check for any faults that might creep into their game.

Just one or two last points before you start building your own set-up routine: concentrate on all of your *four* main sections and give yourself plenty of time to work on them. As you practise and grow more accustomed to the routine, the quicker and more natural it will become. Great players take between one and one-and-a-half seconds to swing, but the set up should take between 10 and 20 seconds when it becomes automatic. Don't worry if it takes 30 seconds at first – as it becomes more familiar, it will get quicker.

Opposite: You can learn a lot about the set up and the swing by watching how the top professionals do it. They take time setting up and may have a few practice swings before they hit a shot. Nick Faldo, shown here, has worked hard at developing a consistent set up and swing. Like other professionals, he can concentrate on the task in hand and mentally block out the crowds around him as he swings.

1 The clubface

In this part of the set up, once again you can break it down into *four* main areas:

1 The target line

Like most good players, you should stand 5-10 yards behind the ball so that the ball is between you and your target. Now try to visualize a line between the two. This process of identifying the target line, although a simple routine, is a very important part of the set up. It is also important psychologically and helps you to think positively, focusing exclusively on the ball and the target, and not on any negative aspects such as water hazards, bunkers, out-of-bounds and other hazards.

2 Placing the clubface 'square'

I would like you to develop a routine of placing the clubface behind the ball with your right hand at the bottom of the grip. The reason for this is to prevent the clubface moving when you commence taking up the grip.

A 'square' clubface means that the bottom edge, or 'leading' edge, of the club is placed at an angle of 90 degrees.

Above: Always place the clubface 'square' to the ball at an angle of 90 degrees.

Below: Place your right hand at the bottom of the grip to prevent moving the clubface.

Above: Make sure that the ball is positioned in the middle of the clubface to provide the best conditions for perfect impact.

Right: The toe of the clubface should be sufficiently off the ground to enable a small coin to be inserted just below the toe of the club.

3 The ball in the middle of the clubface
This may sound obvious but it is very important because you are trying to create the conditions for perfect impact during the 'set up', and to do this, you must strike the ball in the middle of the clubface.

A ball addressed at the heel of the clubface makes you move away from the ball on the downswing to get it back to the middle of the clubface, whereas a ball addressed at the toe of the clubface makes you move towards it on the downswing in order to get the ball back in the middle of the clubface. These extra movements in the swing are not necessary and should be avoided.

4 The toe of the clubhead should be off the ground
When addressing the ball with the clubface, the toe of the clubhead should be off the ground as shown in the illustration, just enough to allow a small coin to fit under the toe. The reason for doing this is that the shaft flexes towards you on the downswing, thereby making the clubhead flat to the ground at impact. The other important objective is to keep your hands just below the level line as illustrated. If this is not possible, get the lies of your clubs checked; this normally happens only with people below 1.6m/5ft 4in or above 2m/6ft 5in in height.

Clubface points to remember:
1 Target-line.
2 Clubface square with right hand.
3 Ball in middle of clubface.
4 Toe of clubhead off the ground.

2 The grip

The grip is the most important feature of the whole of the technical side of golf. When you go through your grip routine and can perfect it, with a little bit of practice, you will start to feel that the golf club is almost an extension of your body – something you can 'feel' throughout your swing. This is the great players' last line of defence in the downswing: even if they are in the wrong position just before impact, they have the capacity to feel and recover from a bad swing and turn it into a good miss, and you are only as good as your missed golf shots.

The left hand
1 The fingers

Continuing on from the clubface routine, you are now standing with the clubface square and your right hand at the bottom of the grip. Take the left hand in an open position and place it behind the grip as shown in the illustration, with the back of the grip in the middle finger position and the little finger 2.5cm/1in from the top of the grip. Once in place, allow the fingers to wrap around the grip.

2 The left hand pad

Once the fingers are in place you must allow the upper part of the left hand to wrap around the

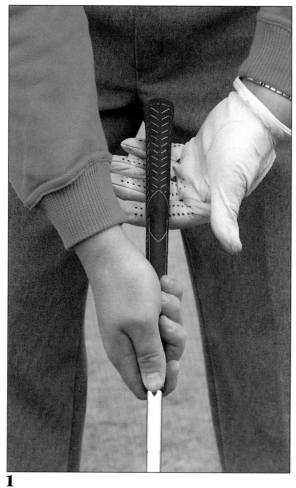

1
Above: Lay the club into the mid-knuckle point of the left hand. The ridge at the back of most grips will then drop easily into it.

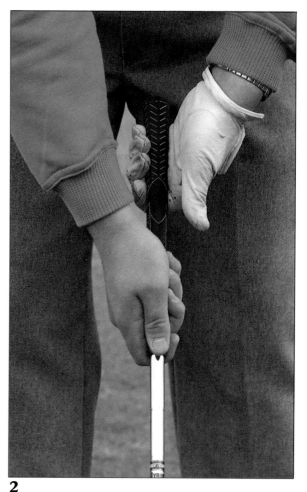

2
Above: Now wrap the fingers of the left hand around the grip of the club.

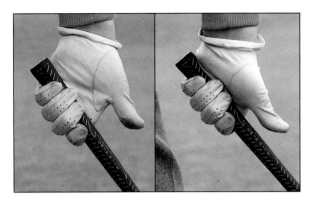

Above: These photographs are the mirror image of those below seen from a different angle.

shaft, so that the left pad is now wrapped around the top of the shaft as shown.

3 Left thumb position

Once the fingers and the pad of the left hand are in place and forming a solid wrap around the top of the grip, place the left thumb so that it points down the top right-hand quarter of the grip as illustrated.

Make sure that the left thumb does not become too 'long', meaning too far down the shaft; it should be shortened so that the pad of the thumb is on the grip.

4 The line of the left hand

The 'line', or 'V', of the left hand is the line

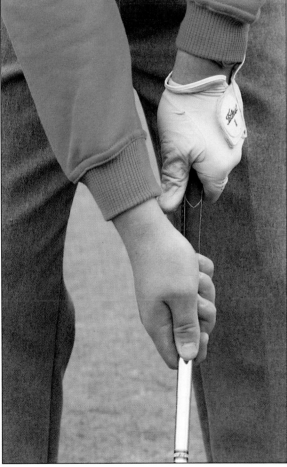

3

Above: Wrap the upper part of the left hand around the shaft of the club so that the left pad wraps over the grip and clasps it.

4

Above: Place the left thumb pointing down the top right-hand quarter of the grip, with the 'V' in line with the right shoulder.

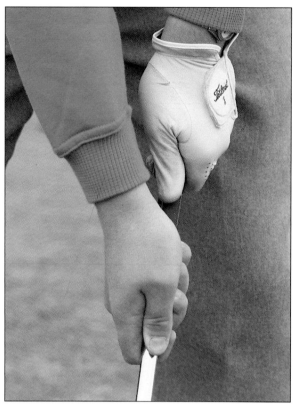

Above: This close-up photograph focuses on the final position of the left hand and shows it placed in the correct position on the grip.

Note: As you progress in your golf career, you may be able to 'weaken' the line of the left hand downwards, so that it points halfway between the right shoulder and your chin. Doing this will help to cut out the possibility of hooking the ball.

Points to remember:
1 Fingers.
2 Pad.
3 Thumb.
4 Line or 'V'.

Above: Make sure that the left hand line, or 'V', points straight up to the right shoulder from the left thumb and the left side of the palm.

created by the side of the left thumb and the side of the palm, once your grip is in place. The line in your left hand points towards your right shoulder as shown in the illustration.

The right hand

Just like your left hand, the right-hand grip has *four* parts to the movement.

There are two main types of grip: the overlapping, or 'Vardon', grip, and the interlocking grip. The interlocking grip is ideal for people with small hands, while the 'Vardon' grip is more suitable for those with larger hands.

1 The fingers

Your right hand is still at the bottom of the grip after keeping your clubface still while gripping with your left hand. Now open out the right hand and allow it to slide up the grip, placing it so that the grip is in the middle knuckle point,

as shown. Now allow the little finger to overlap, or interlock, with the index finger of the left hand as shown in the illustrations.

2 The 'life-line'

Once the fingers of your right hand are in place, wrap the palm of the right hand over the thumb so that the life-line of your right hand is over your left thumb. Make sure that the thumb is in the life-line from the top to the bottom.

3 The right thumb

Now place your right thumb on the top left-hand quarter of the grip, so that the pad of the thumb is on the grip and the left edge of the thumb is just touching the tip of the right index

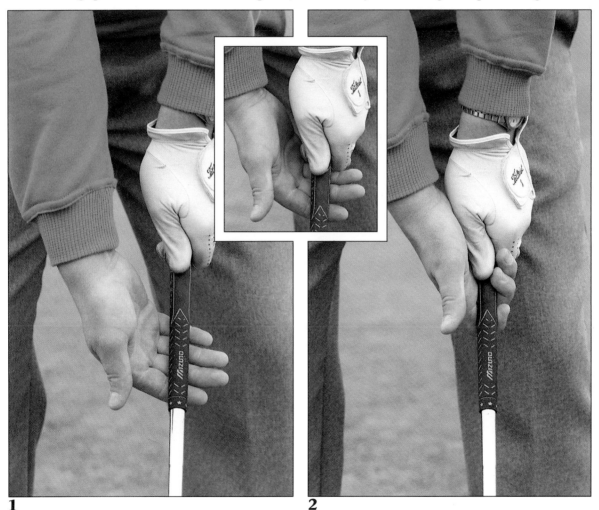

1
Above: Place the club in the mid-knuckle point of the right hand, and move it up the grip towards the left hand (inset photograph).

2
Above: Now overlap, or interlock, the little finger of the right hand with the index finger of the left hand as shown in the photograph.

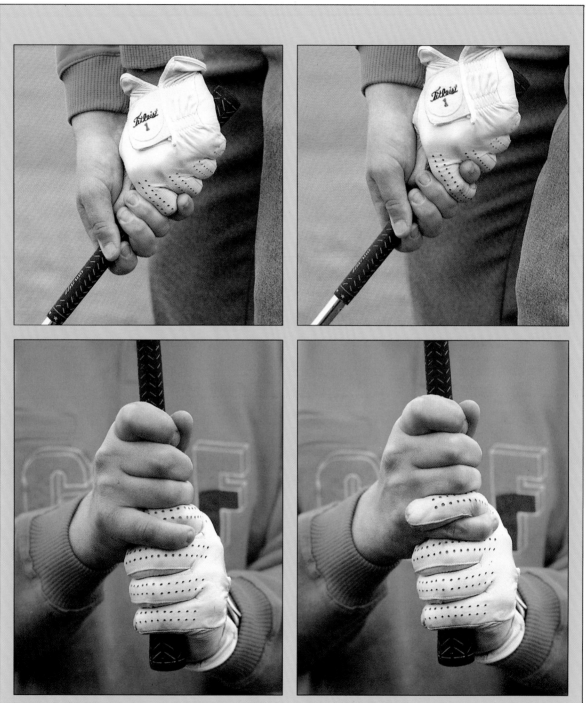

Above: The Vardon grip – the little finger of the right hand overlaps the forefinger of the left hand. This is used by people with medium to large hands.

Above: The interlocking grip – the forefinger of the left hand interlocks with the little finger of the right hand. This is used by people with small hands.

finger. This 360 degrees wrap around the base of the grip will soon start, with practice, to give you a positive feel of what the clubface is doing throughout the golf swing.

4 The line or 'V' of the right hand

As with your left hand, the right-hand line or 'V' should point towards your right shoulder, therefore making both lines, or 'Vs', parallel.

Points to remember:

1 Fingers.
2 Life-line.
3 Thumb.
4 Line or 'V'.

Summary of both hands

Left hand	Right hand
1 Fingers	1 Fingers
2 Pad	2 Life-line
3 Thumb	3 Thumb
4 Line or 'V'	4 Line or 'V'

Note: Make sure that you remember all four points for each hand.

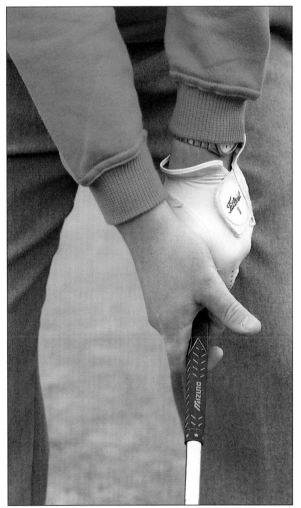

Above: When the fingers of the right hand are in position, the lifeline of the right hand should cover the left thumb from the top to the bottom.

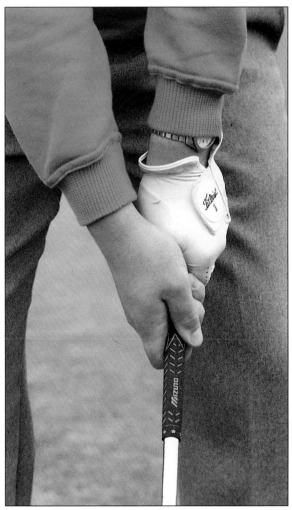

Above: The right thumb covers the top left hand quarter of the grip, creating a 'V' or line with the right shoulder, parallel to the left hand line.

*Above: Here you can see clearly the right hand line,
or 'V', pointing towards the right shoulder with
both lines parallel to each other.*

The stance and ball position

Once again, in the stance you have *four* main objectives, which are as follows:

1 Distance.
2 Left foot (ball position).
3 Left foot (splayed).
4 Right foot.

1 Distance

Now that you are gripping the club and the clubface is in position, you must go into the stance routine. Place both of your feet together, heels, toes and knees at 90 degrees to the target-

Above: Stand with both feet together, knees slightly flexed and, together with heels and toes, at 90 degrees to the target line. If the feet are at less than 90 degrees, there is a tendency to aim to the right and the ball position will be too far back. With an angle of more than 90 degrees, the ball position will be too far forward and then there is a tendency to aim to the left.

Top: You should allow the butt of an iron to drop 4-5 inches above the left knee.
Above: You should allow the butt of a wood to drop 4-5 inches above the left knee so that the length of the club's shaft governs the distance between you and the ball.

line that you created in the clubface routine. Allow the knees to flex slightly, while keeping the clubface behind the ball. Then allow the butt of the club to drop (while still gripping) onto the left thigh. The correct distance from the ball is when the butt of the club is 10-12cm/4-5in above the top of the kneecap. This distance remains the same with all the clubs in the bag, from the 1 wood or driver, which is the longest club, to the sand iron, which is the shortest.

When practising this routine, you should check for two common faults:

1 Too much or too little flex in the knees, which will give you a bad reading of distance.

2 On checking the position of the butt of the club on the left thigh, the golf ball should stay in the middle of the clubface. Otherwise, this too will give you a bad reading of distance.

Right: In this position, there is the right amount of flex in the knees, so that you are now exactly the right distance from the ball.

Above: Too little flex in the knees, thereby bringing you too close to the ball.

Above: Too much flex makes the club ride up the leg, moving you further from the ball.

2 Left foot (ball position)

The movement of the left foot is very important in your set up because it governs the ball position in your stance. You are going to learn only two ball positions: one for all the irons; and one for all the woods.

The irons: The ball position is 10-12cm/4-5in inside the left heel, so allow your foot to travel this distance from the feet-together position, keeping the foot square to the target-line. Think 'heels', *not* 'toes'.

The woods: The ball position is either on the left heel or up to 2.5cm/1in inside the left heel, so just allow the left heel to travel fractionally from the feet-together position, once again keeping the foot square to the target-line. The reason for the exactness of the routine is that you are trying to create two totally different reactions in the impact position.

If you look at the illustration, you can see that the lowest point the clubhead gets to in the downswing is point A, 5cm/2in inside the left heel. The irons are placed at point B, thus allowing the golf ball to be struck first and then your divot of turf, also creating backspin or underspin on the ball. I am often asked how top players achieve backspin and it is as simple as making sure that the ball position is correct.

With the woods the position is completely different. They are placed at point C while the ball position is slightly after the low points, therefore imparting slight topspin on the ball. This is why a top professional's golf ball drives forward with a low penetrating flight, and why when the ball lands on its first bounce, it seems to shoot off due to some of the topspin left on the ball.

Note: Skying, or 'popping-up', your woods is a very common fault that stems from having a ball position that is too far back in your stance with the woods. This causes a downwards blow and also an equal and opposite reaction: hit down – goes up.

Below left: The ball position for irons is 4-5 inches inside the left heel.
Below: The ball position for woods is on the left heel or up to 1 inch inside it.

1

Above: Here the feet are placed together at 90 degrees to the target line.

2

Above: This is the ball position for an iron club with the left foot square.

3 Left foot (splayed)

Once your left-foot ball position is completed for either your irons or the woods, and having kept the foot at 90 degrees to the target-line, just allow the left foot to splay 15-20 degrees open.

This will enable the club to clear your body on your downswing, and allow the clubhead to get through the ball to your intended target. When this does not happen and the foot is retained square to the target-line, it causes you to 'block' the ball straight out to the right, i.e. the body is in the way, and the clubhead cannot follow down the target-line.

4 Right foot

The right foot's main functions in the stance are: to govern the width of the stance; and to help the body stay still in the backswing. Once the left foot has been splayed, then the right foot moves to finish off the stance routine. Firstly, with a short iron, say a wedge or sand iron, allow the right foot to move 15-17cm/6-7in and make sure that it stays at 90 degrees to the target-line. Also think of the heels; it's the width between them that matters. As you work through the iron clubs, 9, 8, 7 and through to the long irons 3 and 2, add 1cm/½in to the width of the right foot. For example, with a 2 or 3 iron the total width is about 37-40cm/15-16in between the heels.

With the woods – 1, 3 and 5 are the usual woods carried by a club golfer – the ball position is on the left heel to 2.5cm/1in inside the left

3

Above: The right foot is moving off square to finish the stance. This varies in width depending on the length of the club you are using.

4

Above: The left foot is splayed 15-20 degrees to enable the club to clear the body on the downswing and to hit the ball on the target line.

heel. Therefore your right foot will have to travel further; with the 5 wood, a distance of about 35-38cm/14-15in. Add 1cm/½in to the 3 wood, and 1cm/½in with the driver so that the distance between the heels with your driver becomes 42-45cm/17-18in, which is about average 'shoulders width'. The reason for this is that the length of the shafts gets longer, and therefore you will experience more leverage with the bigger clubs and you will need more of an anchorage from your stance.

It is very important that your right foot is at 90 degrees to your target-line because in the set up you are trying to create the perfect impact. If the right foot is positioned correctly, then the knee of the right leg will act as a prop in the

backswing and help you to keep still, while turning the shoulders. As Lawrence Farmer will tell you in the chapter on the swing, the shoulders wind and unwind around a stationary head. If the right foot is splayed out, it causes the right knee to bow in the backswing and your head will laterally follow, making a return to perfect impact much more difficult.

Before closing this section on the stance it is important that after the feet have been spaced out you check that your toes are aligned just to the left of the target (about 5 yards away). One very easy way to do this while practising, is to place a club on the ground pointing 5 yards to the left of your target and then to make sure that your feet are an equal distance from the club.

4 Your posture

This means the shape and form of the body at the set up, not just from one angle, but from two: sideways-on; and straight-on.

The straight-on balance line is commonly known but the sideways-on position is not, yet it is 10 times more important to you in your posture. This is because when you either fall away or fall towards the ball while swinging, it has a terrible effect on the golf shot. With the straight-on line of balance, it is possible to sway laterally off the ball and be able to recover and sway back in the downswing, and this does not have such a devastating effect on the shot.

So how do you go about building good posture in your set up? The *four* points to remember are:
1 Left shoulder.
2 Backside (away from ball).
3 Knees.
4 Toes wiggle.

1 Left shoulder

When most good players have finished setting up their clubface position, grip and stance, you will notice that they come up and stand very tall to the ball whilst not moving their feet. This is the start of their posture routine and is a good move for you to copy. The first movement in creating good posture is making sure that your shoulders are on line to the target. You know that your feet are because you have checked this in your stance, but it is easy for your body alignment to spiral open or closed. You need in a good set up to align all parts of the body to the target and they are as follows: feet, knees, hips and shoulders.

To make sure that the left shoulder is on line to the target, once you are standing tall, look at your target and check that the tip of your left shoulder is between you and the target. If your shoulder is to the right of your target, then your shoulders are closed, which often causes hooking and pushing right. But if the shoulder is left of the target, which is an open position, it

will cause a slice or pull left of the target.

2 Backside

Once your shoulders are on line you must concentrate on the balance lines in your posture as already shown in illustrations. The next movement is to push your backside away from the ball until 80 per cent of your weight is on your heels and the remainder on the balls of the feet. It is also important to make sure that your shoulder line is level with the line of the toes, as illustrated. You should now feel that your body is in an angled position with the shoulders and toes in line.

3 Knees

After completing position 2, your next move-

Far left: Shoulder to the right of the target, making the shoulders closed.
Left: Shoulder to the left of the target, making the shoulders open.
Below: The perfect shoulder alignment.
When you look at the flag, your left shoulder is between you and the target.

Top: Push your backside away from the ball, but do ensure that the shoulder line stays level with the line of the toes.
Above: In flexing the knees, the weight is spread 50:50. The hips should not move back excessively towards the ball.

ment is just to flex the knees so that your weight is then spread 50/50 on the heels and balls of the feet. Whilst performing this movement, try to make sure that the shoulder line does not move, and that the hips do not move back towards the ball too much. This movement will give you a feeling of 'sinking' in the lower body. You may also feel that you are tipping away from the ball a little bit, but as 90 per cent of golfers are too much over the ball this will be a good thing. This is why so many weekend golfers fall over or towards the ball in the down-swing, and have to step forwards, unable to hold a full finish at the end of the swing.

4 Toes (wiggle)
This last exercise in posture is purely to make sure that the weight distribution in your body is correct, and that there is no weight on your toes. Top-class professionals can be seen to do this at the end of the set up. They often wear white shoes, which are easy to line up in the stance.

The toe movement is also a way of relaxing before the start of the swing, as some people fidget with their hands and lose a good grip, or move the feet around and lose good alignment in the stance. Just let the toes wiggle up and down; it is a good discipline, relaxing and will not spoil your good set up.

Set up checklist

1 Clubface	1 Target-line	
	2 Clubface square	
	3 Ball in middle of clubface	
	4 Club toe off the ground	
2 Grip:		
Left hand	1 Fingers	
	2 Pad	
	3 Thumb	
	4 Line (right shoulder)	
Right hand	1 Fingers	
	2 Life-line	
	3 Thumb	
	4 Line (right shoulder)	
3 Stance	1 Distance	
	2 Left foot (ball position)	
	3 Left foot (splayed)	
	4 Right foot	
4 Posture	1 Left shoulders	
	2 Backside	
	3 Knees	
	4 Toes (wiggle)	

Summary

The checklist gives you a simple summary of the complete set up. Your main thought pattern should become: clubface, grip, stance and posture. If you ever wonder why even the top players, working day in and day out on their golf games, can hit bad shots, the answer is that the majority of bad shots originate from errors in the set up, which compound in the swing, to give sometimes not just one bad type of shot but several assorted shots, finishing both left and right of the target.

One of the reasons why golf has become so popular is that it has the ability to stimulate both mentally and physically. The set up is part of the mental discipline of the game. As you can see, it is extremely complex in its detail, but, with practice, it will soon become automatic so that you will not even think about what you are doing.

As you develop and fine-tune your set up you will be helping yourself to create more of a perfect impact at set up and also getting your body into an athletic position where it will have greater freedom of movement.

The set up is a development of good thought patterns and physical application that takes time, so don't be too hard on yourself if you have to work on it to get it right. The more you practise your set up the better the bad shots. Just keep remembering the key words: Clubface – Grip – Stance – Posture.

Chapter Three

The Swing

Lawrence Farmer

1

Above: The swing using a driver. Your swing is only as good as your set up. You should relax at address with the head and upper body positioned behind the ball. You should be well balanced and your weight should be distributed evenly between both feet. Before you hit the shot, check that your grip is correct, your feet, hips and shoulder are parallel, and that your clubface is on the ball to target line. The ball should be positioned just inside the left heel. Keep your knees slightly flexed and your hands neither too low nor too high. Your legs should feel supple, not wooden, and ready to play an active role in initiating the swing.

The backswing

The start of your backswing is a very important movement and should be studied carefully. To enable you to understand it better, I am going to describe the backswing movement in two parts: the first part is the takeaway; and the second part is the rest of the swing upwards which will be made easier when the first part is correct.

The takeaway

The start of your takeaway is initiated by your left shoulder pulling your arms, hands and club in a one-piece movement under your chin, whilst your right side turns away from the ball. The first part of the backswing is completed once the left shoulder has reached the chin and the club is opposite the right hip.

Because the left shoulder has moved across to the right under your chin, your body weight will also have moved across to the right. However, you should make sure that the weight stays on the inside of your right foot. It is wrong to throw all of your weight onto this foot since it makes it very difficult to get the weight back off the right foot soon enough in the downswing. The photographs show front and side views of the takeaway.

There are two very important positions that I want you to study in these pictures. The first is the position of the head; you will note that it has not moved at all. I will explain this important position in more detail later on, when the swing reaches the top of the backswing.

Note also the clubhead position. This needs to be studied more carefully because it is critical to the rest of the swing. You will see that the head of the club is pointing correctly to the sky. It is a common fault for beginners (and also among some competent players) to attempt to keep the clubface square to the ball as they swing away, and when they reach the position opposite their right hip, the clubface is pointing down towards the ground. This bad position can feel comfortable to this point in the swing but, once you continue onwards, it becomes impossible to get into a good position and the fault gets progressively worse. However, in the correct

Above: The takeaway is initiated by the left shoulder moving across to the right under your chin. The head stays still throughout.

position, as shown, the clubhead will allow you to continue the swing upwards more freely.

You will also note that the left arm is still firm but the right arm has started to bend inwards, with the right elbow pointing towards your right hip. The left arm should stay firm throughout your backswing. This will give you the correct arc to your swing.

Continuing the swing upwards

After establishing the correct position in the first part of the backswing, you must now continue the swing upwards with the left arm, while, for the first time in the swing, the wrists begin to break and end up underneath the shaft of the club giving a good support. The shaft of the club is then pointing on a line to the target. This wrist action is described as the 'cocking of the wrist'. Your right arm gradually folds until your right elbow points downwards towards the ground.

The firmness of your left arm and your grip will allow your wrists to work naturally. Thus, cocking of the wrists is a natural movement and not something that should be done deliberately.

At this point I would like to refer back to the other important position that I mentioned in the section on the takeaway and that is the importance of keeping the head still. When your head remains still, it is your guide to how far back you can swing the club. Do not be fooled into thinking that a full swing back is when the club, at the top of the swing, is parallel to the ground. This is not so in most cases. You may see many top professional players reaching this position, but remember that they do it every day and, as a result, their

4

5

bodies are more supple than most. This position puts tremendous strain on your back, so please give yourself a period of time to find out how far back you are capable of swinging. Do not rush at it, but work at it gradually until you achieve the best position for you. Most golfers reach what is described as a three-quarter swing, depending on the suppleness of their bodies.

This is a very acceptable position. Once you go beyond your natural top of the backswing position, you will expend a great deal of energy trying to recover it. You need all the energy available to you to hit the ball, so don't waste it elsewhere.

At the top of your backswing, your feet attempt to remain firm to the turf but you may note that a movement of your left foot has occurred. Your left foot should have rolled inwards with the weight falling on the ball of the left foot. Again, this is acceptable, but do not allow it to move too much.

Above and opposite: As you continue the swing upwards, the wrists start to break and finish below the shaft of the club, which should be pointing along the target line. You may only reach a three-quarter swing instead of a horizontal club position.

Tempo of the backswing

The tempo of your backswing, i.e. the speed with which you swing the club back, is also very important. Remember that when you reach the top of the swing, you have got to come back down again so what is the point of rushing it and doing it too quickly? You should go at your natural pace – not too slow and not too fast – certainly no faster than the pace at which you can control the clubhead. Good tempo and rhythm will come naturally from a good backswing and these will influence the pace of the downswing.

6

The downswing

The start of your downswing can be a very simple movement if you start it down the correct way. There are many examples of how you should start the swing down, but the best and simplest way is to initiate the movement with your legs. You will find that if you make a lateral movement of your legs (i.e. take the weight across to the left leg), you will notice that the swing of the club has already started and, more importantly, is moving downwards on the correct attack at the ball – an inside attack.

It is important that you find certain trigger movements in your swing to help the other positions happen automatically almost without you noticing them. If you start the swing down with either your shoulders, arms or hands, this can create a problem in the way your weight is transferred. Your weight will be thrown back on to the right foot, thus going in the opposite direction to the way in which you want the ball to go. Obviously, you want to get the most out of your shot, and therefore both the club and your body must be travelling in the same direction – towards the target.

Once the legs have started the swing down, the hands and arms take over to deliver the clubhead back to the ball. This is done by uncocking the wrists, while the arms are continuing to swing the club down. Your left arm, once again, has maintained its firmness, giving you a good arc width to your swing. This, in turn, allows you to build up a good speed of the clubhead which is needed to propel the ball a long way. Your right arm is still bent, but it has started to straighten out. This straightening of the right arm produces more clubhead speed.

You are now nearly at impact position, and it is essential that you understand the importance of the feet whilst all this is going on. From the top of your backswing, your left foot immediately returns to the turf. This, of course, is perfectly natural because of the lateral movement of your legs. From now on the feet stay in contact with the turf until you are through the impact area. Your feet are the foundations of a good and solid swing, and you should try to keep them in close contact with the turf as

7

much as possible. Do not attempt to throw the weight off the right foot too soon but, instead, let this happen naturally. I will explain in the follow-through how this is done.

Tempo of the downswing

And now for the final part of the downswing, which is the speed at which it should be executed. Because the swing down starts with the legs, this enables you to start down at a comfortable pace and to gradually get faster until the wrists start to uncock, delivering the clubhead at tremendous speed to the ball.

The impact area

The impact area is the most important part of your swing, and your knowledge of this area is the key to your ability to become a good golfer and play to a higher standard. It is easy for me

8

9

to tell you what is the correct position at impact. The left side of your body will turn a fraction to the left, but as long as your arms, hands and, most importantly, your clubface arrive back at a square position, this is quite acceptable.

Please note that the right arm, in the impact position, should still be slightly bent inwards (towards your right hip). This is because maximum clubhead speed will not be reached until the right and left arms become straight for the one and only time in the swing, and that occurs just after impact. The feet are firm to the turf (with maybe a slight rise of the right heel).

The final part of the impact position which I want to examine is your posture. You will notice that the posture of the body at impact should be the same as it was in the address, and therefore it should remain the same throughout the back-swing and also throughout the downswing. If you can achieve this, you will have a well-balanced swing.

Above and opposite: You should initiate the downswing with your legs by transferring the weight across to the left leg as the club moves downwards to attack the ball. As the arms continue downwards, the wrists uncock and your left arm gives your swing firmness and arc width. The right arm straightens to produce more clubhead speed. Your feet should now stay in contact with the ground through impact, giving your swing a solid foundation.

One question that is commonly asked, and sometimes badly answered, is what should you feel you hit the ball with – is it the right hand or the left hand or anything else that comes to mind? My answer to that is: everything is used in hitting the ball. Your whole body works as one to hit with everything as hard as you can. You should not allow any one part of your body to be dominant.

10

11

The follow-through

I would like to separate the follow-through into two parts as described below.

First part of follow-through

From your impact position, you must now allow the club to continue to swing freely until it comes to a halt at the top of your follow-through. This can be made easier when the correct position is reached opposite your left hip. What you must realise is that from now on everything will be like the backswing, but in reverse. This is, of course, what the follow-through is, but with a couple of extra movements to help release the stored-up power. This will take the strain away from the back, hips and neck.

From the impact area, the body and the club turn to the left. As I stated earlier, both arms straighten just after impact to give maximum power through the hit.

Please note the position of the clubhead when it reaches the position opposite the left hip. You will see that the clubhead is, again, pointing to the sky. As I stated in the backswing, this position of the clubhead is extremely important. It is a common fault for many golfers to attempt to keep the clubface square to the hole, but when your body turns to the left so does everything else and this includes the clubface and the path of your swing, which should not go out to the right. You will note that from this position, the left arm bends slightly downwards and the right shoulder comes through under your chin, just as the left shoulder goes under the chin on the backswing. Your right shoulder is an important factor of your swing in the follow-through because this keeps the swing

12

Above and opposite: The club continues to swing freely through impact until it reaches the top of the follow-through. Immediately after impact both arms straighten to give maximum power. When the clubhead reaches a position opposite the left hip, it should be pointing towards the sky. Your body turns to the left and your right shoulder comes through under your chin, and your chest and hips are facing the target as you finish the swing.

on a very wide arc through the hitting area and high into the follow-through. Now your body has turned fully to the left and your chest and hips should be facing the target.

From this position, a couple of extra movements can now be applied because of the tremendous power generated through the hit.

Second part of follow-through

The first extra movement is that, as the right shoulder pulls under the chin and through, you should allow your head to rise up as the shoulder hits the chin. This will then free the swing to carry on to a higher finish. The other movement is with your right foot, which is pulled up onto the toes because of the right side pulling up through into the follow-through.

Please do not try to keep the head down too long – this is another common misconception. The 'head up' situation is caused by earlier faults in the swing. The head should rise naturally to allow the right side to come past the left side into a full finish.

Your left arm, in the follow-through, bends downwards with your left elbow pointing to the ground. This helps to improve your balance at the finish of your swing. Just because the ball has been hit, do not think that the swing has finished. A good, balanced finish is important because you have achieved the swing with speed but you still have control of the club right to the end of the movement.

You may note that at the end of the swing, for the first time, your body posture has changed and your back can straighten up. This is an acceptable position because considerable strain would be put on the body if it was to stay at the angle you adopted at the address position, whilst swinging through at speed into the follow-through.

At what speed should you swing through the hit and into the follow-through? The easy answer is that it depends on your proficiency and how confident you are in your own ability. Obviously, the faster you promote your swing through the ball and into the follow-through, the further the ball will travel. You may have noticed that some top players appear to be swinging the club slowly but still hit the ball a long way. You may also have seen somebody who exerts far more energy but hits the ball a shorter distance. Believe me, to hit a ball a long way the clubhead has to be travelling very fast, but because the swing has a wide arc it tends to give the illusion that the player is swinging slowly.

1 **2** **3**

Swing improvement exercise

Finally, I would like you to understand and practise what I consider to be the best exercise for improving your game and controlling the ball. You may have noticed when watching low-handicap golfers playing that all their swings look different. Well, to a point, this is true, but when the swing reaches its crucial point – through the impact area – most swings are exactly the same. Each golfer's club arrives at the ball on a good line and the clubface is square to that line more often than not.

This leads me to an exercise that you should practise – with or without a ball.
1 Swing the club back to hip height on your backswing only.
2 Now swing down again through to the height of your hips on the follow-through. Practise this continuously, like a pendulum.

Train regularly at this and learn the move-

Above: This swing improvement exercise will help develop ball control and improve your swing. Adopt your usual set up position and swing the club back to hip height. Swing through the impact position to the height of your hips on the follow-through. You can practise this exercise with or without a ball.

ment well. You will soon feel the freedom that the correct movement gives you. All the great players perform this part of the swing well. By practising this exercise, you will give yourself a chance to become a better player.

If after reading this, you still do not understand certain parts of your swing, don't be afraid to visit your local golf professional and ask for expert advice. He can assess and analyse your swing and help to identify and remedy any swing faults. Remember that the better you understand the mechanics of the swing, the clearer your own objective will be, and your swing will soon improve.

Opposite: Curtis Strange winds his upper body into the golf swing by moving his left shoulder behind the ball to get in position for a powerful downswing attack on the ball. His downswing is then loaded with power and accelerates through impact. His weight shifts on to the left side and he finishes in a perfectly balanced position.

THE SWING

Nick Faldo at the point of impact. Notice that he has cleared the left hip, his head is behind the ball and he has fully transferred his weight to the left foot. He is a tremendously powerful hitter with amazing clubhead speed as it accelerates through the ball.

Opposite: There follows a photographic sequence of the swing using a four iron taken from the front and side views. No matter what club you are using, your set up position stays the same for every shot. The only alteration you might make is to narrow the width of your stance as you move down through the clubs from the driver to the wedge. As you study the swing of Ricky Willison, a Great Britain international amateur, notice the backswing, downswing, impact position and the follow-through and finish.

1

2

3

4

5

6

7

8

9

10

11

12

Chapter Four

The
Long Game

Tony Moore

You may not think that your local professional golfer has his own favourite players, but that is where you would be wrong. We all have our favourites. Luckily for me, I was able to watch my four favourite exponents of the long ball game at St Mellion – twice! We had the best four-ball the world could produce in 1988 and 1989. Course designer Jack Nicklaus, without question the finest golfer of the last two decades, was here with Tom Watson, whose simplicity of swings was excellent. Watson's rhythm, technique and timing make him a truly outstanding long game player.

The Americans were pitted against Nick Faldo, arguably the best golfer in the world today, and Sandy Lyle, a past winner of the British Open and the US Masters. It was interesting to watch their technique. Faldo is a player who is technically exact, plotting his way around the course to set up lots of birdie chances. You may not be able to match Faldo's ability but there is no reason why you cannot plan out your long game and think positively too. These are qualities that should be instilled in all golfers from day one. Think positive and you will be positive. This maxim applies, most importantly, to the long game.

You can also do what I still do, and that is to study the style of the world's top golfers. We can all learn so much from their game, long and short. Simplicity is the key, for women as well as men who can drive a good ball. One of the finest swings I have ever seen was Sally Little's, who was at St Mellion for the Weetabix Ladies Open in 1987. She belied her name on the course, with a large appetite for good golf. She hit the ball solidly and accurately, a hallmark of all great players.

Britain's most popular woman player, Laura Davies, had just returned from winning the American Ladies Open. Laura was still suffering from jet-lag when the St Mellion tournament started, because she had had to play an extra day in the United States, but that did not stop her launching the ball a good 280 yards down the fairways. It was interesting to see the women play and, as I pointed out to my pupils, especially my women players, there was something to be learned from watching the top twenty or so women in action.

Finding the right club

You do not have to be physically strong to hit a good drive. It is a lesson of which more men should take heed. Swing the club well, hit the ball accurately and you will achieve a consistently good distance on the fairway. You do not have to attempt to smash the skin off the ball! One of the most common faults, if not *the* most common fault, with beginners using a driver is that they forget how difficult a club it is to use. The actual club has insufficient loft making it a devil to master. This often results in the swing becoming steep and narrow as you try to get the ball up in the air. Timing is ruined, and the final shot is a low slice.

Experienced golfers want a straighter clubface with which they can achieve more distance. But the same rule does not apply to players just starting out and, as we have already learnt, it is only you yourself who can improve your game and not necessarily the clubs you use at this stage. Finding a club with the correct loft is the solution. A club with an 11 to 12 degree face is better than, say, a club with a 7 to 10 degree

Opposite: Sally Little is one of the best drivers in women's professional golf. She has a fine swing and can hit the ball both accurately and solidly. Many women can benefit from using fairway woods instead of long irons as they do not possess sufficient strength to generate enough clubhead speed to hit the ball a long way.

slant. Another good idea is to choose a metal-headed wood. Although it sounds like a misnomer, you should not underestimate the ability of this club.

When Nick Faldo won the Open Championship at St Andrews he used his number two metal-headed wood club most of the way round his final, winning round because of its accuracy. Okay, he may not have been able to hit the ball quite so far with this club, but he was able to position the ball for a much easier route to the green. You all know how good Faldo is, so what is good for the world's best must be good enough for you. I suggest that you look for a metal wood with a 10.5 degree face, and onwards. That will get you in the right direction. Don't forget that if you need help with your club selection, consult your professional – that is why he is there! He will always be able to assist in making the right choice of club for you.

Addressing the ball

As they say, it is different strokes for different folks but there are some basic requirements for us all. Now that you have found the right club, you should set yourself up in the address position to be able to hit the ball slightly on the upswing. This applies to the wood, normal or metal, and the long iron. It does not vary.

From the fairway, with a *wood*, the ball should be swept away with a wide arc, hitting it very slightly on the upswing. In fact it is the same sort of shot we play off the tee with a long iron.

The number one and two *irons* are the ones that we use off the tee, as opposed to the four, five, six and onwards, which are irons struck downwards. But with the number one and two irons, you should try and keep a wide arc and connect the ball on the upswing. Therefore, you should tee the ball up slightly higher than you would for the short irons. Think of your one and two irons as 'driving irons' and, basically, if you use them as you would a driver, you will not go far wrong. Because the shaft is longer – that is why they are called long irons – there is more of a similarity between these clubs and the driver.

Bear in mind that clubhead speed is respon-

Above: Addressing the ball with an iron. With long irons, you tee the ball up a little higher than for short irons and hit the ball slightly on the upswing.

sible for giving you distance. Lurching forwards and chopping the ball in an attempt to kill it creates a high shot. if you are hitting into the wind, you will also get backspin and lift. So, remember to stay behind the ball, swing through with good clubhead speed and you will hit the ball a long way. If you are in doubt, look at how the masters do it. There cannot be many better one-iron players than Sandy Lyle. Watch him take a one-iron off the tee!

Overswinging

A common fault that I often see with new pupils or beginners is that they tend to overswing. The most galling part about it, and one that makes me smile to myself, is that they often get back to a good position. But then they take the club that little bit too far back. Unfortunately, instead of allowing the club to be delivered into the hitting area, for the wrists to be used with a natural, reflex action, it makes you throw from the top with a recoil action. This means that your clubhead speed is at its maximum just past hip level and slowing down at impact. This also causes the weight to stay on the back foot, and often beginners will hit the ground too far behind the ball to have any effect.

Right and below: This sequence shows the common fault of overswinging in which the club is taken back too far, causing the clubhead to slow down at impact and hit the ground too far behind the ball. **1**

2

3

Fairway woods

I am always astounded by the number of new pupils who have quite a good, basic knowledge of the game. However, you can bet your bottom dollar that someone, once a week, and maybe on one of their first few lessons, will ask about the dreaded fairway wood.

There is no real need to be scared off by this part of the long game. Like all other shots, you should assess how you want to play the shot. First, look at the lie. If it's reasonably good, take a number three wood. If it's not, or if it's tighter, take a number five. The most important thing is not to get underneath the ball. Have the confi-dence that you can swing straight through the shot. Again, the wide arc will gather the ball and send it on its travels. The ball will gain its own elevation without you scooping it up for lift. The number five wood has a higher flight than a number three iron and can carry you over troubles more easily. But the number three iron, with its shorter shaft, hits the ball lower and with more control.

Below: Using fairway woods. Work at achieving a smooth, shallow, sweeping action before contacting the ball (below), rather than a descending blow (below left) which gets underneath the ball.

Hitting with and without a tee

When you get your swing organised and it becomes repetitive, there is not much difference between hitting with or without a tee. Basically, you hit through the ball on the fairway, gathering it through the hitting area, whereas you hit it more on the upswing off the tee.

Off the fairway, take sufficient club to make the ball lift. In other words, do not be too ambitious and choose a club which may prove difficult from a particular lie. Do not be over-ambitious; keep it simple, assess the shot before playing it, don't try and whack the skin off the ball and, now I'm going to give you another of my most common lessons, *don't rush!*

One of the biggest faults, and it is not just beginners who are guilty of this, is first-tee nerves. Of course, this fault afflicts beginners more than most, but it also affects us all, at times, making us rush our first shot, which can be the start of a bad round.

There is no point in getting the opening shot of a round over as quickly as possible. It is your most important shot, but this does not mean that the world is watching you. Try and forget that there may be others looking at your start. Probably they are just as worried about their own opening gambits, and invariably they are more interested in their own game, so you should concentrate on yours.

Having selected your driver, you must tee up. In ideal conditions, position the tee so that half the ball is showing above the club-head. This allows for the swing to sweep the ball, striking it slightly on the up and allowing the ball to find the centre of the clubface.

If the wind is blowing into your face, position the ball a little lower in order to create a penetrating drive. Now that you've got the picture, you will understand that if there is a following wind, you tee the ball that little bit higher, but do not alter your shot. The wind will carry the ball naturally without you hitting it even harder than usual.

As a beginner, or if you are more experienced and want to play for safety, use a three wood from the tee. Tee the ball up so that just over one-third of the ball is showing above the club-

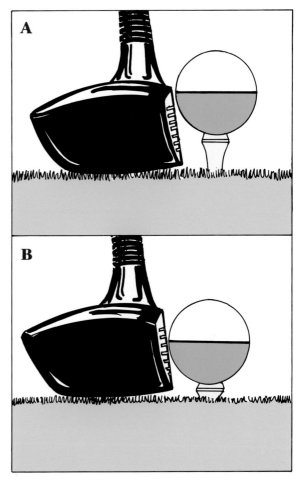

Above: The illustrations show how to tee the ball for driving (A) with half the ball above the clubhead; and into the wind (B) with the ball positioned slightly lower.

head. You should do this because the additional loft on the clubface, which I have already mentioned, makes contact well below the equator of the ball, creating backspin and loft. To aim the shot, pick a spot on the fairway where you want the ball to pitch. Remember also that it may run on, so take this into account.

Again, for beginners, I always suggest that they tee up in the centre of the teeing ground, between the ball markers. Professionals can shape their shots by varying their starting point but you will learn this later as you become more experienced and skillful.

Above: In order to aim the ball with accuracy, try to visualize your intended shot. Select a 'marker' on your line of flight and aim through the line with your feet aligned parallel to it, and the clubface positioned behind the ball.

Aiming the ball and visualization

After teeing up, stand behind the ball and select an object such as a small tuft of grass or flower on your intended line of flight. This should be between two and four feet in front of the ball. Position the clubface behind the ball and aim through the line you have selected. Your feet are then aligned parallel to this line.

By concentrating on your 'marker', the flower or whatever, you will not be thinking about possible hazards ahead and therefore your address position should be just right for a decent drive. When you are waiting by the first tee try and relax as much as possible; tension will lead to terrible shots.

A good way of relaxing before a round is by warming-up. This does not have to be too strenuous and the following exercise is quite simple. Put a club behind your back, hold it between your elbows and turn 90 degrees on the backswing and then 90 degrees on the follow-through.

Above: A simple warm-up exercise is to hold a club behind your back in your elbows and turn the hips and shoulders to the right, then to the left, to *stretch out the muscles and thereby to simulate the action of the golf swing.*

1 **2**

Another good way of releasing tension is to get two clubs and swing them backwards and forwards, loosely. This helps loosen up arms and wrists as well as breaking those arthritic cracks which invariably accompany the first few swings of the day!

Mentally, the most important thing about a solid long game is to be positive and picture yourself making a good shot. Commitment to a good swing results in a good swing. Do not let your mind become too flooded with the difficulty of the shot, the wind factor and so on. Clarity and simplicity are the two things on which you should concentrate.

It is a discipline to which you must commit yourself if you want to play a good game. Just visualize yourself playing the right shot; imagine that someone is taking a photograph of you making a perfect swing and playing it.

Of course you should also bear in mind that the course architect has designed the course in such a way that you are tested. The plan is to punish the unwary, and the over-ambitious, but

Above: Another good loosening-up exercise is to swing two golf clubs loosely backwards and forwards holding one in each hand.

reward the prudent and cautious golfer who plays the course as it was designed to be played.

The art of designing a course involves selecting and creating features at each hole, measuring them from tee to green and collating them into a yardage chart, or 'cheat sheet'. The information gleaned from this booklet is of great importance but you must remember that the distances are measured from the centre of the fairways. So either you should play a superb straight game and stick to the book, or find out the hard way about judging distances, which is what most of us have to do. Playing your home course regularly and getting to know its peculiarities will give you an advantage when it comes to competition.

You may learn, for example, that the bunker on the left side of the fairway is only a seven iron from the green on a calm day and that a tree on the right-hand side of the 10th hole is where you usually land with a well-struck drive and so on.

One thing of which you should be wary is whether the pin position on the green has changed. If the green is 30 yards long, a normal length, then you must plan for stronger clubs if it is at the back rather than at the front on your approach. This sounds simple, but it is surprising how many people take it for granted that the pin will stay in the same place.

Although you should not cloud your mind with hazards, you must be aware of them. For example, if there is a sand trap down on the right of the fairway, you should approach it with caution. Say that it is about 200 yards away and you hit your best shot, but will it carry over the bunker? Does it help to pass the bunker by 10 or 20 yards? The cross bunkers just short of the green will still be too far away to negotiate.

By now you know my policy: simplicity and safety. Play short of the sand trap, then take a medium iron and lay up short of the next hazard. Try to plan the best position for you to set up the next shot which you feel, like all your other shots, is within the compass of your ability.

It is no good approaching a par five with a double figure score already on your card after you stupidly got over-adventurous at the last and landed in that second sand pit. The principle is the same with that mammoth par five that you are now approaching. Do not be overawed and do not be foolish. Just because you saw Ian Woosnam play the same sort of hole in three on television does not mean that you are going to do the same. Instead, be happy to get on to the green in four decent shots and then try and putt out in two – not make the green in two! If you do, you are almost bound to make an air shot if you are a beginner.

That said, if you do make an air shot, just walk away from it, pause for a few minutes and then come back for your second attempt. If I am feeling tense, I often clench my fists tightly on the grip and then release them. Then when I replace my hands I usually have a much more comfortable, and softer, grip, which is conducive to a better shot.

Practising your long game

The long game is physically demanding and requires practice. I recommend that about 20 per cent of your practice time should be concentrated on hitting the longer shots. Then when you are out on the course, you can really enjoy playing this side of your game. Take time in hitting those full shots; it will not be wasted. Some people choose to practise at home without hitting a ball. I think that just going through the swing regularly helps to build up good 'muscle memory' and this can be used to good effect out on the course.

Useful tips for your long game

Back on the course, it is best to remember that it is not all doom and gloom when you start. Enjoy your game, but don't get too carried away with the brilliant shot you have just played. I often see beginners clinging to one 'favourite' club going up the fairway because they have just hit a good shot with it. I try and start all my pupils off with a six or seven iron so that they can become accustomed to hitting the ball sweetly. I never start them with a driver or a long iron because I know that they will lean back on their right foot and probably make all the other mistakes I want them to avoid.

I also ask them to wear comfortable, loose-fitting clothes. As I have said, the long game – the whole game – is a taxing one, and it is no good feeling uncomfortable, at play or practice. The same rule applies to wet-weather gear. Clothes with a generous cut are unrestrictive and will avoid thinking about 'tight fits' when you may have to concentrate on a tight situation!

Talking of wet-weather clothes brings us round to how rain and wind will affect your long game. It is rare to get a perfect day for golf, so learn to use all the elements as your allies. If it is raining, the ball will stop quickly and stay lower, because the wet turf has a 'pull' on the ball – a bit like suction. On a dry day, even if it is baking hot, the ball will run further on firmer ground. If the wind is behind you then, again, you will achieve more distance.

Try not to let the elements distract you from your game; your partners will be experiencing the same conditions, after all. Playing into the wind is difficult for everyone, so make allowances for it. It is not easy but just play a little bit stronger against it. I judge the wind like a clock. If it is blowing from 10 o'clock, when you turn into it, allow for the drift back. In real terms, you are facing it directly so an extra club will be required in order to:

1 Keep the ball lower.
2 Cater for the loss of distance incurred by the force of the wind.

Do not be intimidated by difficult weather conditions: instead, learn to use them to your advantage.

One way of combating the wind off the tee is to use a driver, although I am always reluctant to suggest that players who have just begun should use this heady instrument. Yes, it gives you distance, if used well. However, for anyone not familiar with it, the driver will also get you into far more trouble than any other club. If my pupils have a handicap of 18 or above, I keep them on a two or three wood, which both do the job.

Golf is not about hitting the ball as far as the eye can see. When pupils use an iron from the tee and are unable to use a wood, it is invariably their grip which is at fault. They invariably develop a 'hooker's grip' and find it very hard to change and, therefore, use the woods correctly.

I think that you should always attempt to use woods off the tee initially. The iron may give you safety but, again, it is best to be able to use all of the clubs for their particular job except, at the early stage, the driver. Your professional will guide you in your choice of clubs.

I also think that it is a good idea to go out on the course and play a round or two occasionally with your club pro. He will elevate your game and help you to use the right clubs. It is natural to take the easy option – for example, the five iron along the ground instead of the the pitching wedge – but, with your professional's encouragement, the difficult shots will bear fruitful rewards.

Judging the lie of the ball

Your pro will also be able to explain an important part of the long ball game, apart from club selection, which is judging the lie of the ball. The way the ball sits on the grass can dictate your club selection.

A ball on **a wet fairway** will, when you make contact, have a cushion of water between the clubface and ball. Consequently it will shoot off lower and without backspin, thereby adding about 15 yards to the shot.

In grass **higher than the equator**, the ball will skid off the clubface with a lot of topspin – a 'flier'. The trajectory is lower so a more lofted club is required.

Take an extra club if the ball is teed up well on a **clump of grass**. It may look a welcome sight but it will invariably be the top half of the blade that makes contact and loses you distance.

When the ball is **above your feet**, you will naturally play a draw – a right to left shot – giving it a lot of life on landing. If you want to be cautious, play a club less.

Conversely if the ball is **below your feet** the opposite happens; there is a fade in flight, giving the ball spin and stopping it quickly, so an extra club is called for.

It pays to think about playing to an **elevated green** as well. The ball will hit the slope while in flight, so always take two clubs more than you first thought you would need.

And what about that awful **steep downhill slope** lie? It's the one that all beginners manage to get into, at some stage, and the one they fear most. You may have to take between one and three clubs more lofted than you would normally use, depending on the incline of the slope. To ensure that you make contact with the ball first, rather than the ground, the position of the ball should be set towards your back foot. Keep your stance open, to allow for the slice that will occur from this position. The success of this shot is to maintain a good balance, so adopt a comfortable position with your right knee bent more than your left. Swing your club slowly and try to allow the clubhead swing to follow the contour of the slope.

If you end up in **long grass** you will need the

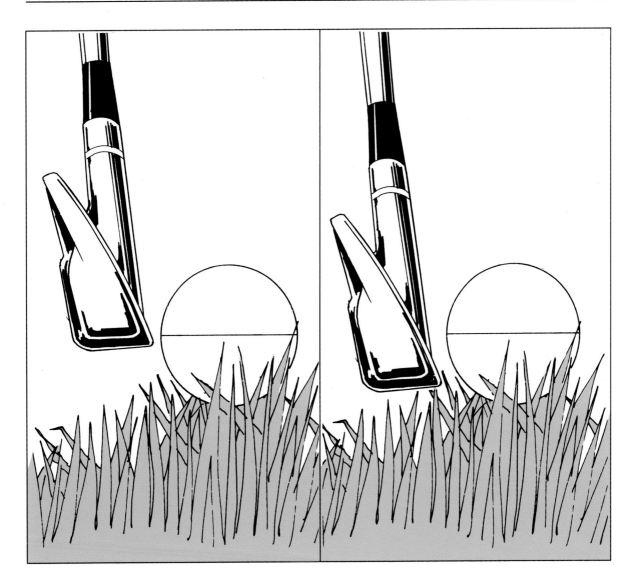

Above: If the ball is teed up on a clump of grass (left), the leading edge of the blade should be level with the centre of the ball. Addressing the ball at normal height (right) may cause a mishit.

same open stance. Open the clubface and position yourself so that the ball is one inch further back in your stance than normal. From this set up you have to swing across the line of flight, gripping your club firmly in the left hand to cater for grass binding around the neck. The stalks, stems or blades can roll the clubface over and smother the shot, which is worth about an extra 50 yards in length if cultivated.

Practice makes perfect

This rule applies to all aspects of the game of golf. I hope that this chapter will improve your long game. Concentrate on these things and on perfecting a clean, straight shot and you will be able to get on to shaping your shot . . . and get down to a handicap where you can begin to master the driver.

Above: How to play an uphill lie on the fairway. The correct way to play this lie is to stand with your spine at right angles to the slope. Flex your left leg a little more than usual and then shift more of your weight onto the right leg.

Above: The wrong way to play an uphill lie. You will not strike the ball well and may strike the ground at impact if you fail to make the adjustment shown (above left). Nor should you swing the clubhead too steeply in this shot.

Chapter Five
The Short Game

Pip Elson

THE SHORT GAME

Without doubt, one of the most satisfying aspects of a round of golf is 'getting out of jail' with a par when the hole has been played badly. It gives you a mental boost walking to the next tee in a medal round and causes irritation and annoyance to an opponent if he fails to win a hole in matchplay that he rightly feels was his.

Many a top professional would admit to the fact that a low score of 67 or 68 has often been achieved by the psychological lift of knowing that he has played poorly on the opening holes only to pitch and single putt well to remain close to par. Conversely, frustration can abound by splitting every fairway and hitting every green in regulation only to see a deserved low score frittered away through clumsiness around the greens, resulting in a bemoaning, 'If only I could putt' and the inevitable 74 or more.

A good short game is vital, not only because it saves shots but, probably more importantly, because of the impact that it has on your mind, which influences the decisions you make on shotmaking during the course of a round. Let us examine the art of scrambling or rolling three shots into two, and the variety of strokes that faces us all at some time or another.

Strategy

All too often I play with friends or pro-am partners and, on reflection, some young pros too, who on the vaguest scent of the green will have their wedge out of the bag to play their next shot before they have even reached their ball. This is a big mistake. There is such a variety of possible shots available which should be examined before a decision is made, that clearly to make a premature judgement is foolish. There are two extremely important pre-shot situations that should be followed correctly.

Firstly, there are certain questions which need to be answered so that the type of shot selected can be played with confidence in the knowledge that the alternatives have been dismissed as unwise. Every pitch shot from 100 yards and closer will always be assessed carefully by the experienced player. How is the ball lying, which direction is the wind blowing, where is the pin position, is the green receptive or not,

how am I swinging today, how will the ball react on pitching? These are all questions that must be analysed before you make a decision. Remember that you are looking for the percentage shot, the shot that you feel will 'come off' more times than the alternatives. Unless circumstances dictate a gamble to go for the pin tucked behind a bunker from a bare lie because you are two down, then the percentages must always be obeyed. In the long run this will be the best policy. We all like to talk about the spectacular shot that occasionally makes the 19th hole *après golf* banter marginally less boring than usual for the assembled gathering. But remember that your companions, too, will have a similar tale to relate from their recently completed rounds. The company all too sadly will have one thing in common. In attempting to beat the odds, everyone knows in their heart of hearts that four or five shots have been wasted in similar situations before the successful one ensues. These, naturally, are conveniently not mentioned!

Secondly, the importance of a consistent routine cannot be stressed too highly. Because most shots from within pitching distance depend on good 'feel' as well as technique, it is vital that the pre-shot routine is not disturbed. Watch any good player, and the time between taking the club out of the bag and striking the ball is amazingly constant. This is because all the questions in the previous paragraph have been answered correctly and there is no indecision as the strategy has been worked out before the club is selected. The remaining time is spent creating the necessary feel to judge where the ball will pitch and then how it will react on landing. An extra glance up at the pin or a waggle of the clubhead can often ruin the flow of the shot.

Backspin

Before we move on to the various techniques and common faults of the short game it may at this stage be worth explaining one small point concerning backspin. I will explain how backspin is applied later on, but all long-handicap amateurs are green with envy as they watch golf on television and see the professionals pitching their ball by the hole, taking a bounce forward only to spin back and nestle close to the flag.

I have played with captains of industry who would willingly sacrifice the company Jaguar car or Caribbean beach house to just once see a ball 'back up' on the green.

Your choice of golf ball determines to a large degree the amount of backspin imparted when struck. The harder two-piece ball favoured by amateurs for its durability and small length advantage has up to 30 per cent less spin velocity than the softer balata covered ball used by touring professionals. This will obviously cause the occasional shot to 'jump' or shoot off the clubhead, making the control of this particular type of ball more difficult with extra roll on landing more than likely. Unfortunately, although the ego may be boosted if some balata covered balls are purchased to help achieve this lifelong ambition, the bank balance certainly will not. Any mishit will result in an ugly cut in the softer cover and the inevitable opening of another packet of three!

Judging distance

Of all the different headings under which I have written about the short game, judging distance has presented me with probably the biggest challenge. How do you judge distance? I have concluded that there is only one answer. That, of course, is practice. Practice of the right kind is essential. It gives the correct feel and also the necessary experience of how the ball behaves when struck from different distances, heights, lies and wind direction. Of course, it also teaches you what happens when it pitches on the varying conditions of the green.

How do you judge anything? Let's tackle the question. Are you a good judge of people? If the answer is yes, then why? Surely it's because you have met a lot of people in work, leisure or social occasions – in other words, experience or practice. How does a shopper know whether something is a good buy? Again, the answer must be by being aware through experience of the price and quality of the articles. The art of judging distance in golf – and it is an art – must come

Above: The art of judging distance is one of the most important aspects of the short game. Jack Nicklaus is a master of this art.

from being able to simulate the distance in a disciplined, thoughtful practice routine. I well remember how I created my own as a youngster by opening an umbrella on the practice ground and placing balls at about 9m/10yd intervals up to about 91m/100yd, and trying to pitch into it. Not only was it creating feel but it was also good fun. It taught me perhaps my greatest ever lesson in the art of judging distance in the pitch shot: simply, never decelerate. (Never decrease the speed of the clubhead as the club approaches the ball in an attempt to judge the distance.) This, above anything else, is where in my experience of playing with the handicap golfer, far too many of you make mistakes. Most commonly it is overswinging that causes this gravest of errors.

Pitching

Before I bury too many 'don'ts' in your mind, perhaps it is now time to examine the 'do's' that encompass a good action and will lead to the shot saving we all desire, on and around the green. 'Feel' and judging distance are without doubt absolutely vital, but without sound technique they can be a wasted asset.

The 'do's'

As with any shot in golf a good set-up, i.e. aim, grip, stance and posture, is a basic necessity in the pitching action. However, there are three slight modifications to the address position that may help to improve striking the ball:

1 The weight should be just a little more on the left side.

2 The hands should always be ahead of the ball.

3 The ball should be positioned in the centre of the stance.

This leads to a swing that will create a crisper descending blow into the back of the ball, thereby helping to impart backspin with a ball/turf strike culminating in better control. One of the secrets to this shot is in attempting to keep the upper body still, especially the head, and trying to use mainly hands and arms. This will create a good feel for the shot and also the correct balance with the legs playing the important role of weight transference. Any lifting or swaying can lead to inconsistency and result in hitting behind the ball or a 'fat' shot or, just as bad, topping or 'thinning' the ball.

Below: The correct position for addressing the ball (left) with the weight fractionally more on the left side and the hands ahead of the ball. The wrong position (right) with the weight anchored more on the right side.

1

2

The short pitch. When pitching you should set up with an open, but narrow, stance. The shaft of the club and left arm should form a straight line. Swing quite steeply, keeping your head steady. Let your hands lead the clubhead on the downswing. Try to keep your head steady and the upper body still – your hands and arms will do the work.

3

4

As you swing the club back, some weight will be transferred automatically to the right leg. Then the weight will be transferred back to the left leg as you swing the club down and through. Use your legs to give your swing rhythm and to swing through without the clubface closing.

5

6

The loft on your club will lift the ball into the air, so there is no need to help it. Keep the clubface square through impact and afterwards to impart maximum backspin on the ball with a ball/turf strike. It is essential to be in control throughout the pitching action.

7

8

At the end of the swing, the arms swing to the left side of the body which now faces the target. At the finish, the back of the left hand and the clubface should face more towards the sky than towards the ground.

Above: Many golfers attempting a pitch shot spoil it by overswinging. When pitching correctly, the clubhead should be accelerating at the moment of

impact, but by overswinging you reduce the speed in the hitting area. This leads inevitably to poor shots that miss the target.

The 'don'ts'

I have always believed in letting the loft of the club do the work, having seen so many golfers fail by trying to lift or scoop the ball with a premature uncocking of the wrists during the downswing. Unless the ball needs to have extra loft, i.e. to be hit over a tree, immediately on leaving the clubface, this is a definite mistake. A slightly more open clubhead position and stance should be adopted in this instance to help create the required height, with a more

outside to inside swingline in order for this to be achieved.

Lastly, the most common fault amongst amateurs spoiling this shot is to overswing. Instead of ensuring an accelerating clubhead at impact, the overswinging golfer will reduce speed in the hitting area causing faulty judgement of distance and inconsistent striking. To cure this error will take a few practice sessions disciplining yourself to swing the club at least as far on the throughswing as it was swung on the backswing.

3

4

Above: Overswinging can create faults in your judgement of distance and cause you to lose control, thereby missing the target completely. If you suffer from this problem, you should practise swinging the club at least as far on the

throughswing as you swung it on the backswing. Spend some time on the practice ground perfecting your technique for pitch shots until you can strike them consistently and accurately.

The pitch and run

I have been fortunate enough to have played golf on a variety of courses all over the world. Without doubt, though, there is no greater test of skill than the challenge of a British seaside course in breezy conditions. It examines every department of the game, places great emphasis on strategy and gives enormous satisfaction when a good score is achieved. It is to me the ultimate test in the conditions in which the

Above: When you set up for the pitch and run, you should adopt a similar stance to that used for the ordinary pitch with an open, narrow stance and the weight slightly favouring the left leg. You usually play this shot with a six, seven or eight iron.

game was originally meant to be played. It takes years of experience to understand and accept the cruel bounces, difficult lies and varying skills that will doubtless be encountered on a links course. There will be one sudden realisa-

tion during the first experience of seaside golf, which is, of course, that the game was never meant to be fair.

A pitch to six feet on an overwatered green with the ball stopping dead pales into insignificance against the skill and guile it takes to perform and execute the pitch and run over the humps, hollows and slopes of the seaside course to a similar distance.

The pitch and run can only be played under certain conditions, but is indeed a friend to have

Above: In the hitting zone, you should take care to keep the blade of the club square. Keep your left wrist firm and do not allow the right wrist to become over-active or roll over before striking.

in the golfing armoury. It should only be attempted if there is no rough or coarse grass between the ball and the flag. On a windy day it helps to keep the ball down and minimizes the effect that the wind has on the flight. It is

5 **6**

usually played with either a number six, seven or eight iron. The art, of course, is to judge how far the ball will roll forwards on landing and then the effect of any contours of the apron and green. Half the skill is deciding when the pitch and run shot should be used; indeed, a lofted wedge may often be preferable. However, I do feel that for the handicap golfer it is an excellent percentage shot. There is far less margin for error in the simple half swing which is all that this shot requires.

Above: On landing on the green, the ball will roll forwards, and by practising this shot, you will soon develop a feel for it, and will be able to judge the distance that the ball will roll on landing.

A similar stance should be adopted to the ordinary pitch, but care taken to keep the blade square in the hitting zone with a firm left wrist, not allowing the right wrist to become over-active or to roll over prior to the strike.

7

8

Above: The finish of the pitch and run. The ball lands on the green and rolls towards the flag. Any contours on the apron and green will affect the

direction of the ball and should be taken into account when playing the shot.

Chipping

I have always felt that when playing any shot from around the green the hands should be placed a little further down the grip, perhaps an inch or two nearer the shaft. With a slightly more bent-knees position, this has always given me a better feel for the shot in hand, especially for judging the distance. One of the greatest exponents of the short game I have ever played with is Ken Brown. This was very much the method he adopted, and indeed on occasions his right thumb and forefinger were actually on the shaft!

From the apron: The chip shot can be a saviour, and if played correctly it can be made to look simple. Selecting the correct club is very important. Many players have a 'favourite' club they always use and even though it sometimes may not be the right choice, the fact that this enables them to play the shot with confidence usually over-rides using the wrong club. Fear of failure to execute a relatively simple stroke probably causes more indecision and poor results than lack of technique ever does. By just taking a little more time to work out the type of shot you are attempting, you may build up the confidence to hit the ball correctly. Judging how the ball will react on landing is perhaps the key to a successful chip. Once again the importance of a firm left wrist through the hitting area cannot be stressed too much, and, of course, slight club-head acceleration at impact is critical. A straighter-faced club other than a wedge should be chosen for this shot as the ball will have a flat trajectory and, on hitting the putting surface, will roll forwards a considerable distance.

From the rough: Perhaps a common sight to you all every Sunday morning is that of one of your four-ball fluffing a chip from the semi-rough by the side of the green. The ball might go only a yard or two, but in order to avoid this happening, you should heed the following advice. There should be an earlier cocking of the wrists on the backswing than for a normal shot. This will create an immediately steeper take-away resulting in a sharper descending blow into the back of the ball, thereby ensuring that a fluff is eradicated.

At the address position, the ball should be more towards the right foot with the clubface a fraction open. At impact the club should be accelerating through the ball, with the swing-line slightly from outside-to-in. A wedge or sand wedge should be used for this shot.

One important point to note is that a chip shot from the rough will always run further than one played from short grass. This is because more often than not the longer grass will be 'wedged' between the clubhead and ball, reducing the effect of backspin because the effect of the grooves on the clubface will be partially negated. The same effect can sometimes be experienced when playing in wet conditions. We often hear the term 'a flyer'. Wetness will have similar results on the flight of the ball to that of long grass, causing loss of backspin and leading to lack of control.

Above: The photographic sequence shows chipping from the rough. At address, the ball should be more towards the right foot with the clubface fractionally open. The ball should be positioned back in the stance. Cock the wrists earlier than normal on the backswing to create a steeper takeaway and a sharp descending blow into the back of the ball which will avoid catching the club on the grass. The club

should be accelerating through the ball at impact, hitting down and through so that the ball will fly low and run further than a normal shot played from shorter grass. Longer grass may get 'wedged' between the clubhead and the ball, reducing the effect of backspin.

Above: The photographic sequence shows chipping from the apron. Unlike the chip from the rough where you use a wedge, for this shot you should use a straighter-faced club as the ball will have a flat trajectory. Set up with your feet quite close together, bending slightly forwards from the hips with your weight more towards the balls of your feet. This gives you more space for your arms to swing

through freely. You must keep the left wrist firm through the hitting area with the clubface facing the target. The left hand must not stop nor try to scoop the ball but keep moving through towards the target. Keep your head still until after you have struck the ball.

The Texas wedge

This is the term that is used to refer to a stroke from off the putting surface where the putter is used. It is, in my opinion, perhaps the most under-used shot by the high-handicap player. Many of you think that it is imperative to chip a ball from just off the fringe, but this is a nonsense. If ever there was a percentage shot, this is it.

A bad putt will *always* work out better than a bad chip. It's true, isn't it? Ask yourself this question: how many times after a bad chip shot have you scolded yourself for not having taken a putter? A chip you could have hit just in front of your nose or, just as bad, clean through the green. It does not have to look pretty – just get you the right result. There is no particular method in playing this shot differently to that of a long putt. However, as the distance between yourself and the pin is likely to be quite a long way, it is important to approach the shot correctly.

The ground between you and the start of the putting surface should be reasonably smooth and flat so that initially the ball has less chance of bumping from its intended line. Having decided to play the Texas wedge do not stand over the ball too long in the address position. This can cause you to lose the feel of the distance. Having had a couple of practice swings with the putter in an attempt to judge how hard to actually hit the ball, a couple of looks at the hole is all you need having addressed it. The longer you stand over the ball the less likelihood of producing a satisfactory result. This pre-shot routine is the same as for a long putt from on the putting green.

Above: Sometimes you may have to use your putter to hit a ball from off the putting surface onto the green. This shot, known as the Texas wedge, is seldom used by beginners and high-handicappers but it can work out better than a chip shot. To play the shot, the ground between you and the green must be relatively smooth and flat so that the ball will run along its target line without deviating. Play the shot as you would a long putt.

Putting

How can it possibly be right for a player to strike a magnificent drive 250 yards followed by an imperial long iron to the heart of the green of the most difficult par 4 on the course, only to see all this effort wasted with a frustrating three putt?

Ideally on fast greens, a putter should be quite light giving more feel for the judgement of distance. On slower greens, a heavier putter will help to ensure that not too many putts are left short.

The grip

I have seen many different ways in which people grip the putter. It is the one club in the bag that the teaching manuals are not too dogmatic about how it is held. I have known famous players use two or three different putters during a tournament with varying grips too!

The one rule that I feel should be followed is to grip the putter in a way that binds the wrists. This stops either hand from dominating as the putt is struck. An involuntary last-second 'hit' with the right hand is perhaps the most common error leading to inconsistency in judgement of distance and putts being missed both left and right.

To avoid this, the most popular way of gripping the putter is to stretch the index finger of the left hand over the four fingers of the right hand, thus ensuring that the wrists are locked during the swing of the putter. This is known as the reverse overlap grip.

The stance and stroke

How you stand to the ball when addressing a putt is again a matter of personal preference. Open, shut, wide or narrow are all acceptable and there is no hard and fast rule. Michael Bonallack, now secretary of the Royal and Ancient, in his heyday as an amateur was one of the most formidable figures to wield a putter in the world of golf. His ungainly wide stance, and resulting ugly posture over the ball, was his well-known trademark. But my goodness, were they

1

2

Above: The reverse overlap grip. Place both hands on the grip with palms either side and the thumbs on the front of the grip. Take the left index finger off the grip to overlap the four fingers of the right hand and create freedom of wrist action.

effective! Ask David Kelley of Blackwell Golf Club who was on the receiving end of the Bonallack magic in the final of the English Amateur Matchplay Championship over twenty years ago at Ganton. He holed this difficult course in 73 in the morning round yet stood an incredible eleven down at lunch. The moral of this is that if it works – stick with it.

This ridiculous scenario has caused many a swear word, divorce, broken club, lost tournament and, on occasion, even giving up the game. The putter, however, is without doubt the most important club in the bag. I would be the first to admit that having a good short game and consistently good results with the putter were the backbone of my abilities on the professional tour. Mark James once described me as a 'hot dog' pro. In other words, if I hadn't been able to putt I would have been selling hot dogs at the 9th for a living!

There have been many arguments about the emphasis placed on the importance of putting for as long as I can remember. Enlarging the hole to reduce the good putters' chances of competing is perhaps the most commonly voiced. Never! Do that and the game will lose its traditions, resulting in the authorities being blamed for trying to make everyone equal. Golf was never meant to be so. Many different kinds of designs of putters have been made in an attempt to improve scoring. Most of us have a few putters locked away that 'might just do the trick' if the current favourite lets us down. Manufacturers prey on golfers who putt poorly, with marketing ploys to convince them that their 'larger sweet spot' or 'uniquely balanced' putter is the answer to their prayers. But if the truth be known, with just a little practice and a couple of basic principles to obey, all of you can improve your putting results.

Choice of putter

It is very difficult to choose or recommend a putter for someone else. What I like may not suit the next person. However, in general, if you tend to stand a long way from the ball when putting, a putter with a flat lie would be more suitable than one with an upright lie, this being more appropriate for someone taller or a player who stands closer to the ball. There are three common denominators you will find with all good putters:

1 The ball is never positioned further back in the stance than the middle of the feet.
2 The putter always accelerates through the ball at impact.
3 The ball is struck 'on the up', thereby creating an immediate good roll of the ball.

Above and opposite: A good way to read your putt is to crouch down on your toes behind the ball. Assess the line to the hole, the distance and the height of the ground. Look for any slopes that might affect the roll of the ball and try to visualize its path. You should look from the side of the ball as well as from behind to read the green.

The roll

The initial roll of the ball on leaving the face of the putter is vital. If the ball is placed back in the stance, it increases the chances of hitting down on the ball which makes it jump. This can cause a small deviation in the direction and an untrue roll of the ball. All good putters will accelerate the ball at impact and strike it at the start of the upswing. This will help the ball to travel on the intended line with no deviation. This particular method of putting is most effective on good, fast, true greens. Keeping the wrists idle in the hitting area and developing a stroke that involves the elbows being tucked into the sides and a feeling of the shoulders rocking from side to side is, in my opinion, the best way to consistent putting. However, if you can adapt your stroke a little to suit less perfect greens, it can pay dividends.

1

Above: This photographic sequence shows how to putt consistently. For the set up, position the ball in the middle of the feet. Bend forwards from the hips to leave your arms free to move. Your stance should be narrow with the weight evenly distributed, and your head behind the ball. The putter should

2   **3**

accelerate through the ball at impact striking the ball 'on the up' to achieve good roll. Thus you should not have too short a backswing which will cause excessive acceleration and throw the putter off line, nor too long a swing which will slow down at impact. Your elbows should be tucked in to the

sides of your body throughout, and keep your head still. Don't be tempted to look up and see how well you have hit the ball until it is on its way rolling across the green towards the hole.

The rap

I used to reckon that whenever we played a tournament on bad or grainy greens, somewhere close to the top of the leader board would be a South African. This was because he had been brought up on greens where 'nap' or 'grain' played a big part. With the grass being much coarser, a firmer method and a more positive 'strike' or 'hit' of the ball were essential. Gary Player is perhaps the greatest exponent of this style. His wrists break almost immediately on takeaway and the ball is struck almost forcing it towards the hole with little or no follow-through. Gary Player was, and I'm sure still is, a tremendously courageous putter with the ball always being struck firmly into the back of the hole. Never up, never in was his motto.

Try this method on temporary greens or when the normal greens have been allowed to grow a little longer than normal. You will be surprised at how effective it can be.

The dreaded twitch

As yet, I have been fortunate enough to have avoided this awful affliction. However, I have seen it in action. If fellow golfers know you as a twitcher, they will avoid you in the knowledge that you possess one of golf's fatal diseases. Amongst other things it can be brought on by the knowledge of a larger than healthy overdraft or an over-fondness for vintage claret, but this virtually incurable ailment reduces grown men and women to shambling indecisive wrecks of their former selves. This of all golf's trials, tribulations and faults is perhaps the most difficult to shed. I can offer only a modicum of advice. Either try left hand below right which reduces the right hand's influence in the hitting area, or most recently the best anti-twitch technique I have seen is the innovative Sam Torrance long putter.

This involves a very subtle pendulum-type action placing the right hand with only marginal pressure on the grip about 37cm/15in below the left hand. It works for Sam who was once one of the best pressure putters on the Tour. As this putter is approximately 50 per cent longer than any normal putter, you must first overcome the embarrassment of being seen with a club that would appear to be attached to your left nostril when in use!

Reading greens

Judging how much a ball will swing on the green is difficult. Subtle breaks and borrows can fool the most experienced of players. I have always found it helpful to look at a putt from both the side of and behind the ball. This I have concluded gives you a good feel for how much the ball will turn during its roll. It is important to realise that a putt will turn a lot more when it is losing speed or 'dying' at the hole. On a long putt, try to visualize the hole as a dustbin lid, trying to ensure that the second putt is the easier uphill or right-to-left putt rather than the nasty curling left-to-right downhill one.

Summary

The short game will always be the most critical part of golf. Unfairly you might say – so be it. But remember that in a round of 72, the putter can be used anything up to 36 times. Thirteen clubs are therefore used to hit the remaining shots. Need I say more.

Our professional superstars of today are very articulate in post-round interviews, explaining in detail every shot, lie, unlucky break and so on that happened during the previous four hours or so. The importance of the short game was never better summed up than in a subtle comment made by the late great Walter Hagen after one of his many tournament victories. A reporter asked him how many shots he had taken on a previous hole, to which Hagen simply replied, 'Four'. Hoping for a slightly more elaborate answer, the intrepid hack inquired of Hagen how this 'four' was achieved. 'Oh,' he said, 'three of those' – and then with a twinkle in his eye, added – 'and one of them!'

Chapter Six

Overcoming Hazards

Jim Christine

OVERCOMING HAZARDS

You're in trouble – a loose shot has put you in a difficult place. It is absolutely essential that you end up in less trouble after the next shot. All too obvious, you say, but think back to your last round! Did you go for that magical recovery – you know, the one Nick Faldo would not have attempted – and end up in deeper trouble than when you started?

In this chapter, we are going to explore sensible shot selection and techniques to help you escape from various situations. You will learn how to play shots that will enable you to get your ball back into play without sacrificing too many strokes. We will also determine what you should do when a shot is impossible to play, enabling you to make the best decision at all times to keep your score under control.

The importance of the lie

In order to play a successful shot in any golfing situation, you have to have sound technique. However, even with sound technique, you are not guaranteed success if you make wrong decisions and play the shot incorrectly. This is even more true in trouble spots.

You cannot play any shot if the lie does not allow it. Here is your first rule for trouble spots: always play the shot the lie of the ball allows rather than the one required to reach the green. There is no point in deciding that you need a five wood to cover the 180 yards to the green if your ball is lying in a hole at the bottom of a clump of heather. A sand wedge to the nearest piece of short grass is probably the only possible shot.

You may laugh, but in my career as a professional golfer I have seen players trying to play impossible shots all too often.

The rough

In the rough you are going to be faced with an array of situations. Some will play exactly like a fairway shot, as the lie may not prove to be a bad one, but others will be very difficult. Always look at your situation objectively, play within your normal limits, and plot your easiest route to the green. If you always think of hitting the ball as far as you can, most likely you will not be playing the best shot. You will probably end up staying in the rough, in a bunker, or on a piece of ground, making your next shot much more difficult.

Sometimes you may not be able to reach the fairway; however, that does not mean that you just hit and hope. Think – is there any more reasonable ground close by which you can reach? Perhaps there is a place within one or two clubs' lengths offering a good lie, from which you can play after taking a penalty drop. This will give you a decent shot, albeit at a cost, but perhaps not as much of a cost as four or five hacks in an attempt to reach the fairway.

There follows a description of the different sorts of lies you will find in the rough and an explanation of which technique to apply in each situation.

Different lies in the rough

Good lie: You will recognise a good lie when you see one. However, be careful to observe which way the grass is growing. It will only be a good lie if the grass lies in the same direction as you are going to swing.

Ordinary lie: This is the lie that you can expect to experience in the rough most of the time. You can see the ball well enough, but it is low down in the longish grass, and this grass is obviously going to get between your clubface and the ball at impact.

Bad lie: You should also recognise this lie easily, as it will be the one you are left with when you have only found your ball after a lengthy search, nestling very low down and enveloped in long grass, and almost obliterated from view.

Apart from the 'good lie', the other situations are characterized by one thing: the grass in the rough is going to affect your shot. Even when the ball appears to be lying well, the grass may be growing against your direction of play and this will affect your swing and the ball flight. It may look quite reasonable on first inspection, but beware. In these lies, the club's movement will be restricted, sometimes even stopped. This restriction causes:

1 Your clubhead speed to reduce.

2 Your clubface to close, delofting the club and making the ball fly low.

Both of these can be enough to cause you to fail to get the ball out of the rough.

If you are in a good lie, play the ball as if it were on the fairway. For all other situations, however, the approaches described below should be taken.

Club selection

Once you have decided that the lie is more difficult than a fairway shot, you must use your more lofted clubs to play the stroke. I would not recommend an iron above your *seven*; you have to be very strong to keep a six iron or less moving through heavy grass. However, I would commend you towards a very lofted wood with a heavy sole which will prove a better bet that an iron for most club golfers. The more difficult the shot, the more lofted the club should be.

Right: The photographs show a good lie (top); an ordinary lie (centre); and a bad lie (bottom). If you have a good lie in the rough, you may find that it is better to use a wood than a long iron as it can slide more easily through long grass. Again, with an ordinary lie, a wood, with its longer shaft, can move through the grass easier than an iron. If you do use an iron, increase your grip pressure to control the club better. When you are confronted with a bad lie with the ball nestling low down in deep rough, you need a very lofted club, preferably a wedge or sand wedge. Keep your swing short and drive the clubhead down and through the ball to lift it out of the rough and back on the fairway.

Swing technique – ordinary lies

Having selected your club, do you need a particular swing technique to play this difficult shot? The answer is yes.

Irons: Due to the grabbing effect of the longer grass, especially when the grass is wet, you will have to increase your grip pressure to maintain control of the club. As there will be grass behind the ball, you should play the ball slightly further back in your stance, towards the mid-point between your feet. This will have the effect of steepening your angle of attack, which helps you to get a clean hit at the back of the ball. This does not have the effect, however, of decreasing the loft of the club, making your club selection even more critical. Make sure that you choose the more lofted club if you are undecided between one and another.

During the swing, keep your action crisp: a nice three-quarter backswing, followed by a smart hit down and through, will carry you on to a reasonable finish. Do not worry if the follow-through is a little restricted as the club will be held back by the grass. However, it is important to follow through as far as you can.

Woods: With its longer shaft, creating more momentum, the wood has more chance of moving through the grass easily. However, it must be at least the loft of a *seven* wood before it will be a successful shot. Do not be tempted to try shots from poor lies with a less lofted wooden club.

Play with a slight increase in grip pressure, although not quite as much as with an iron. Move the ball back slightly to just inside the forward foot's heel. This time play with a full, free swing to keep the momentum going and trust the club to play the shot up and away to the target.

Above: The address position for an ordinary lie with an iron. Play the ball further back in your stance to steepen the angle of attack. It should be towards the mid-point between your feet.
Opposite: The address position for an ordinary lie with a wood. You should position the ball slightly back just inside the forward foot's heel. Play the shot with a full swing.

1

2

Swing technique – bad lies

These shots can only be played with an iron and a very lofted one at that. You really should be playing with your wedge or sand wedge in these situations. Keep a firm grip on your club, play the ball back opposite your back foot, keep your swing short, and punch the ball to the nearest piece of fairway. It will be impossible to make much of a follow-through, but make sure you accelerate the club into impact.

Heather: When you are faced with heather instead of grass, you can think of the effect that grass has on your club and double it. Heather is tremendously strong, so treat it with great respect. If the lie looks at all difficult, reach for your sand wedge, aim the shot over the shortest distance to the fairway, hold tight and get yourself back on the short grass.

3

4

Opposite and above: This photographic sequence shows the address and swing technique for playing a bad lie with a wedge.

1 Take up your address position with the ball well back in your stance opposite your back foot. Grip the club more firmly than usual to counter the resistance of the grass.

2 The backswing. Make a short, steep swing and

hit down as hard as possible.

3 Just before impact. Literally punch the ball as hard as you can into the air and onto the nearest piece of fairway.

4 The follow-through. Do not worry about distance – the important thing is to get the ball back on the fairway in one shot. Remember that to do this, you must accelerate the club into impact.

Different lies on the fairway

Sloping lies: You will encounter sloping lies every time you go out on the course. Do not over-react by thinking and playing any differently if you are on a slight slope. However, if the ball is on an obvious incline, you will have to adapt your technique slightly, but it is important not to try to do too much. On all sloping lies, concentrate on maintaining good balance and rhythm, and play within your capabilities.

Uphill lies: An uphill lie is one where the ball is positioned on an upslope, sloping towards the target. This is probably the easiest of these shots to play; for the first time you have your own launching pad to get the ball airborne. However, this also brings about subtle changes to your swing and ball flight: your six iron will fly as high as your seven iron and go about the same distance. The slope will also make it difficult for you to move properly through your shot. This produces a tendency for the clubface to be closed on impact, making the ball draw or hook in flight.

To play the shot, it is important to allow for these changes in ball flight and not to fight against them. Aim your shot slightly to the right of your intended target to allow for the hooking, right-to-left spin. To accommodate the slope, move the ball position forwards in your stance towards your higher foot and allow your body to achieve a perpendicular position with the slope by shifting more of your body weight to your lower foot. These adjustments will put your address position back to its normal relationship with the ground allowing you to use your normal swing.

Downhill lies: A downhill lie is one where the ball is on a downslope, sloping towards the target. This is the exact opposite to the uphill lie already described. The slope is now pointing downwards, making it difficult to get the ball into the air. However, it does mean that you will hit your eight iron the same distance as your seven iron and with the same ball flight, so at least playing with a slightly easier club gives you greater margin for error.

Above: Address position for an uphill lie. Move the ball position forwards in your stance towards your higher foot. Shift more of your weight to your lower foot so that your spine is at right angles to the slope before you swing.

Again your first task is to get your club selection correct. Do not even consider your straight-faced long irons from this lie, because you will not get them airborne. Stick to a five iron or a more lofted club.

The downhill slope will again make it more difficult to move properly during your shot; it will make your pivot more difficult on the backswing and therefore create a swing that will tend to make the ball fade or slice. Remember, allow for the ball flight and accommodate the slope.

Above: Address position for a downhill lie. Move your ball position towards your higher foot back in your stance. Put more weight on your lower foot, and set your spine perpendicular to the slope before you swing in a rhythmical way.

Very steep uphill and downhill lies

You are now in a situation where your balance is in real jeopardy. The slope has become so severe that any attempt to get your normal body relationship to the ground would cause you to fall over. All you can do is to play the ball back to a flat piece of ground and start again from there. Any attempt to achieve too much distance from these lies will have disastrous consequences.

In these situations, you need to bend your higher leg at the knee until you feel that your balance is secure. It is very important not to exceed your limits, and to play only small swings with your more lofted clubs.

Your aim and the position of the ball in your stance are the same as when playing from ordinary uphill and downhill lies. Remember that uphill lies cause the ball to fly from right to left, so aim right of the intended target, and you should position the ball nearer your higher foot at the address. Likewise, downhill lies will cause the ball to fly from left to right, so you need to aim left of the intended target, and again you should position the ball nearer your higher foot at address.

Your aim should be slightly to the left of your intended target as the ball will curve to the right in flight.

To reorganise your set up for this lie, you should again move your ball position towards your higher foot. Allow more of your weight to favour your lower foot, placing your body perpendicular to the slope.

Maintaining your rhythm and balance and, above all, playing with a reasonably lofted club, are the keys to success with this tricky shot.

Ball above your feet

Due to a combination of swing path and face angle, this shot will tend to fly right to left in a draw or hook shape. The ball will go about the same distance as normal, but this time the slope has brought the ball slightly closer to you. Accommodate this by moving your hands down the grip of the club a little, making the playing length of your club shorter. This is referred to as choking down on the club. As your swing is going to be more around your body on this lie, lay the ball opposite the middle of your stance, and be careful not to be pushed back on to your heels too much – maintain as much of your normal weight distribution as you can.

Below: Address position for ball above feet. Grip a little further down the shaft of the club. The ball should be positioned in the centre of your stance.

Above: Address position for ball below feet. Notice how the knees are flexed more than usual to maintain balance and get down to the ball.

Ball below your feet

This lie takes the ball further away from you and is inclined to make the shot move from left to right in the air. Allowing for this movement, you must aim slightly to the left of your intended target and, to help reach the ball, you should hold the club at full length.

In complete contrast to the situation where the ball is above your feet, described above, play the ball forward in your stance just inside your left heel. To get down to the ball, you must bend forwards from your hips and then use your knees to maintain balance. This is a difficult balancing position, as it is very easy to fall forwards towards the ball, so no heroics – swing smoothly and keep the ball in play.

Bunkers

Bunkers can make or break a score, so good technique and sensible thinking are critical to minimizing the damage. This section looks at different types of bunkers, the special techniques required to play in them, and how to play out of different lies.

Greenside bunkers

A greenside bunker can be defined as a bunker within reach of the pin in one shot. This will obviously vary between one player and another, so it is important to know your own limits.

This is especially important when considering the height of bunker lip you can expect to clear. Even the best players in the world cannot hit a ball vertically upwards; they know not to try. Learn what you can and cannot do during practice and if needs be come out of a bunker to the side or even backwards, where the lips are not so steep, and you will end up with a lower score.

Club selection

You should play with your most lofted club, the best option being a proper sand iron. The sand iron is designed specifically for use in bunkers – it has a fairly heavy sole with some degree of 'bounce'. This is a technical term describing the angle of bulge on a sand iron – if you compare a sand iron with a pitching wedge, you will notice that the soles are very different, the back of the sole of a sand iron being lower than the leading edge, designed so that the club does not dig too deeply into the sand but slides easily through.

Swing technique: the 'Bunker shot'

Just as the sand iron is designed specifically for bunkers, so is the technique you should use. Unlike an ordinary shot, you do not use your club in the square position. To maximize the loft of the club and hence the height of the ball's flight through the air, you must address the ball

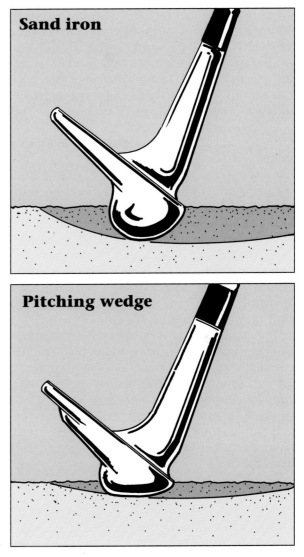

Above: The sand iron has a deeper flange than the shallower pitching wedge, which has less loft and is more suitable for use in bunkers with less sand.

with an open clubface. This means turning the club to the right before you take your grip.

This clubface position has the effect of making the ball fly to the right of where you are aiming it, so you therefore have to take this into consideration when lining up the shot. You should open your stance, aiming the lines made by your toes, knees, hips and shoulders to the left of your intended target. By the time you have opened your stance, the relationship between the leading edge of your club and the target should be back to 90 degrees.

The ball position must be kept in the forward half of your stance, just inside your front heel. You should wriggle your feet into the sand just enough to cover the soles of your shoes. This helps in three ways:

1 It gives you a firm foundation in the loose sand.

2 It gives you a chance to test the surface of the bunker, helping you gauge just how much sand there is.

3 It lowers the base of your swing to below the level of the bottom of the ball, making it easier to get the ball airborne. Now just make an ordinary swing, aiming to strike the sand 5cm/2in behind the ball, and making a good follow-through. The ball will float out on a cushion of sand.

The distance you hit the ball is dependent on the length of your swing, and you must practise to learn your own distances. Keep your strike point constant, because if you try to work with two variables, your swing length and strike point, it is terribly difficult to achieve consistency of distance. You do not vary your strike point on a fairway shot, so don't do it in a bunker either.

Practice drills

To practise the special bunker stance, imagine that you are trying to hit an ordinary straight shot, ten feet to the left of the pin. Having established your stance, relax your grip, turn the club until the leading edge is aimed at the target, retake your grip, and swing. This will help you to get used to the way the bunker position feels and what to expect from the ball flight.

To practise striking the sand 5cm/2in behind the ball, draw a straight line in the sand at right angles to you with your club, making it two to three yards long. Then keep making swings to hit this line. Once you can strike the line consistently, place some golf balls two inches on the target side of it. Now go back to striking the line,

Above: Address position for an ordinary lie in a greenside bunker. Address the ball with an open clubface and open your stance.

Opposite: At impact, you should strike the sand about two inches behind the ball. You should practise this until you can do it consistently.

and the balls will float out of the bunker, giving you confidence in the shot before you try it on the course.

Above and opposite: This photographic sequence shows the swing technique for a normal bunker shot. When you address the ball and line up the shot, open your stance in such a way that the lines made by your toes, knees, hips and shoulders aim to the left of your target. The sand lines indicate an open stance. There should be an angle of 90 degrees between the leading edge of your club and the target.

1 Make a normal backswing, taking into account that the length of your swing will determine the distance you hit the ball.

2 Strike the sand 2 inches behind the ball.

3 Follow through and the ball should get airborne and float out of the bunker on a cushion of sand.

3

Difficult lies: plugged ball, ball in a footprint, hard and wet sand

These are all situations in which the bottom of the ball is below the level of most of the sand in the bunker. You therefore do not want to use the 'bounce' on your sand iron, and a digging action is needed to play these shots.

The leading edge of the club is used to effect this digging action. Unlike the ordinary bunker shot, described above, the clubface in these situations should be in the same position as for a normal golf shot. Your stance alignment should

Above: Address position for a bad lie. Note that the ball position is slightly further back, causing a steeper backswing to get to the bottom of the ball.

also be the same as for a normal shot. One important difference, however, is in the position of the ball in relation to your feet. You should position the ball opposite the middle of your feet with your hands just opposite the inside of your forward thigh. This means that your hands are more ahead of the ball than in a normal shot.

These changes make the arc of the swing steeper, giving you a descending blow, so that the cutting, leading edge gets to the bottom of the ball. This is all you need to play the shot successfully from these difficult lies. You will not be able to make much of a follow-through, and the ball will run on landing, but you will be out of the bunker. Again, your aiming point is a point in the sand slightly behind the ball, and you will have to try some practice shots to see exactly how the ball reacts.

It is usually possible to play the ball from a very buried position, but you will have to learn when to take a penalty drop by your own experience. Try all sorts of positions when you practise to learn just what you can and cannot do. If your ball is really buried, close your clubface, rotating it to the left to make full use of the sharp leading edge, and hit hard in the sand just behind the ball. If you practise and hit it correctly, you will be amazed at what you can achieve!

Fairway bunkers

The thinking that you must employ when playing out of a fairway bunker is similar to playing from the rough. The great temptation is to think distance to the green. This is fatal; instead you should concern yourself with judging which club you need to comfortably clear the bunker lip. Your main objective is to get the ball back into play, better off than you were, in one shot.

Your technique will depend upon the quality of your lie. If the lie is poor, play the shot as if you were in a greenside bunker – heroics will not enhance your position. If the ball is lying well, sitting cleanly in a well-raked bunker where you feel you have every chance to hit the back of the ball, play it as described opposite.

Above: Address position in a fairway bunker. The ball position is normal in the stance. Grip the club more firmly than usual and then wriggle your feet very slightly into the sand.

Choose a club that you feel will clear the bunker lip easily. Your technique must help you to strike the ball first, ensuring that there is no contact with the sand before the ball, thus maximizing the distance you can achieve. Aim your shot in the normal manner, wriggling your feet into the sand just enough to help make a solid foundation for your swing (not as much as in a greenside bunker). The position of the ball in your stance is as normal, but you must firm up your grip pressure slightly. This has the effect of shortening the muscles in your arms a little, and reduces the freedom of movement in your

wrists. Both of these changes will widen the arc at the bottom of your swing, which will enable you to hit the ball cleanly. Keep your swing under control, using a firm three-quarter action, maintaining rhythm and balance throughout your stroke.

Do not try to force the shot – hitting too hard will only make you strike inaccurately, causing a poor shot. If you have chosen the correct club and played the shot smoothly, the only thing left for you to do is to clean up the marks you have made in the bunker and get on with your round.

Above: Make a three-quarter swing and do not strike the ball too hard. Ensure that you do not make contact with the sand before the ball to deaden the strike.

Trees

Almost every golf course has trees as potential hazards. While adding beauty to the course, they can produce ugly results on your scorecard. Here I describe some typical situations and how to cope with them.

Under trees

There are two options here: a low shot under the branches, or a shot through a gap in the branches. Of the two, the former is the more realistic, as trying to judge the ball flight to squeeze through a gap is very difficult.

A low shot is quite easy to play as long as you choose a fairly straight-faced club. Having done that, play the ball back in your stance, opposite the mid-point between your feet, retaining your normal hand position just opposite the inside of your left thigh. The secret is not to hit the ball too hard – play the ball softly, giving it no chance to rise.

As a last resort, you can aim for a gap in the trees, but make sure that you have considered all other possibilities first, including taking a penalty drop. If you do go for a gap, success is much more about club selection than technique. You have to marry the club trajectory to the gap available. Having done this you must play your normal shot, trust the club, and pray!

During these shots, you may experience some interference at points in your swing. If your backswing is restricted in any way, this could prove difficult. However, if you maintain your rhythm and try to keep your downswing very slow, you should succeed in making reasonable contact with the ball. The bad shots come when, having felt the restricted backswing position, you rush the downswing towards the ball at twice your normal speed.

Trees between you and the hole

These are really advanced shots and should not be attempted unless you have tried them with success on your practice ground or driving range. There are three ways of negotiating this situation:
1 You can go over the trees.
2 You can go around the right side with draw.

Above and opposite: Address position for playing a low shot under trees. Note that the ball position is back in the stance opposite the mid-point between your feet, to keep the ball flight low underneath the branches of the trees.

3 You can go around the left side with fade.

If you really want to attempt these shots, get some professional tuition. A more easy option is to play sideways for one shot, getting yourself back in play where you can see the target.

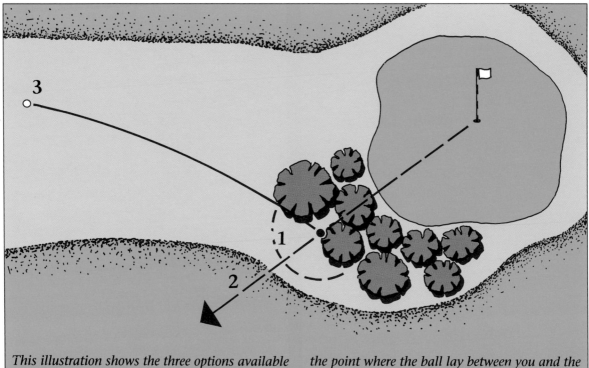

This illustration shows the three options available when taking a penalty drop from an unplayable lie.
1 Drop within 2 club lengths of where the ball lay, no nearer the hole.
2 Go back as far as you want on a line that keeps *the point where the ball lay between you and the hole.*
3 Replay the stroke from the spot where the ball lay before your last stroke.

Taking a penalty drop

A penalty drop seems like the very last resort to most golfers. Do not allow this to be the case for you. Sometimes it is the best route to reasonable damage limitation.

You have three options when taking a penalty drop:
1 Drop your ball within two clubs' lengths but not nearer the hole.
2 Take your ball back as far as you like while keeping the point where it originally lay between your intended dropping point and the hole.
3 Replay your shot from the spot in which it originally lay before your last stroke.

These options all cost you one stroke. This may seem a high price to pay, but often it is the best means of keeping control of your score.

Summary

As you will see from reading about these different shots and situations, the key to successful recovery from trouble spots is to think sensibly and tactically before you attempt anything. It is tempting to go for the most aggressive, attacking shot, and it may make you feel better not to play defensively – but when you suffer the consequences of foolish decisions and add up your scorecard at the end of the round, you will probably say, 'If only I hadn't tried that shot.'

Golf is a game that requires skill and intelligence, and when playing trouble shots, intelligence has to take precedence over your emotions!

Chapter Seven
Curing Common Faults

Nigel Blenkarne

CURING COMMON FAULTS

I am going to tackle the most common faults that beset many golfers in two ways in order to show you:

1 How to identify, define and understand the causes of bad shots. I will give you a checklist of cures for whichever fault afflicts your game.

2 A selection of the basic faults that recur most often amongst golfers of all standards but are particularly evident in beginners and high-handicap players.

The ability to identify your error correctly is half the battle and will greatly simplify your efforts to rectify the problem. In many cases one fault leads to another in an attempt to compensate for the initial one thereby setting up a vicious circle which is hard to break.

The golf swing is not a series of isolated movements; each part is related and connected to the others, and the influence on the swing itself is traced back to the way you hold the club and set up to the ball. *Therefore the more you allow for a fault the more you create and encourage it.*

However, I must stress that every fault can be over-corrected, which is why golf is such a difficult game. I have witnessed many times keen and receptive pupils taking away from a lesson the key points to work on only to find that at the next session I am saying exactly the opposite in order to get back to the correct neutral position. Thus the golf swing is a constant updating and fine-tuning exercise regardless of the length of time you have been playing this wonderful game. This is why top professionals will continually return to their gurus to check their swing and their game. The extent of variation tends to be more pronounced in the less experienced player which suggests that the longer you have been playing with a fault the harder it becomes to make changes, but certainly not impossible! We all tend to have our own in-built faults which we return to when our game goes sour, but once these faults are identified we have a better chance to control and correct them. It is encouraging that given practice, application and the correct thoughts to work with, you can improve and enjoy your game more.

The shape of the shot you hit is a reflection of your swing pattern and the ball responds only to the forces applied to it in terms of:

1 The swingpath.
2 The clubface at impact.
3 The angle of attack.
4 Clubhead speed at impact applied squarely.
5 Contact from the sweet spot.

In my analysis of the following faults and cures I shall refer to these ingredients. There is no magic to golf; we must simply apply logical mechanics, the laws of physics, to our game.

Please note that my descriptions of ball flights and reference to left and right sides are applicable to the right-handed player. My apologies to any left-handers reading this but you need to do the reverse in every instance although the principles are identical.

Opposite: The photographic sequence shows the normal golf swing and the ideal swingpath that you are trying to achieve. The club lying on the grass behind the ball indicates the target line. The club lying on the grass to the left of the ball indicates the line of the swingpath that the ball should follow. Hitting the ball on the correct swingpath is the key to hitting good shots and avoiding the faults that plague many golfers.

The slice

Definition: The ball starts its flight to the left of your intended target line and then curves severely to the right. This is a weak shot which lacks power and often will fly higher than it should do.

Cause: This shot is the bane of most beginners and high-handicap players. Invariably this shot pattern develops through an incorrect grip and hand action which cause the clubface to return to the ball in an open position (aiming to the right of the ball to target line). This causes the ball to finish right of your target, and the natural step when you are on the course is to start aiming further left because you don't want to lose all your golf balls in the trees on the right!

However, the more you allow for your slice the more you perpetuate it. In fact, if you are aiming considerably left then your swingpath is likely to be running the same way and you must deliver the clubface in an open position, or otherwise the ball will fly straight left.

The cure for slicing is as follows:
- The left hand should hold the grip in the fingers, but not too tightly.
- The feet and shoulders should be *parallel* to the target line.
- Your left shoulder should be higher than the right one.
- Do not roll your hands and open the clubface on the takeaway.
- Make a more rounded, flatter swing.
- At the top of the backswing, the clubface should be on the same angle as the shoulder plane.
- Make a full shoulder turn, with your weight on the right leg.
- On the downswing, move your arms close to the right hip.
- On the throughswing, move your arms away from the left hip.
- The back of the left hand and forearm should rotate within the arc of the swing.
- The club shaft must point downwards on the follow-through (clubhead at lower end).

- Your weight should shift onto a firm left leg on the follow-through.

Equipment: pay attention to the following points:
- The lie of the club may be too flat.
- The grip may be too thick.
- The club shaft may be too stiff.

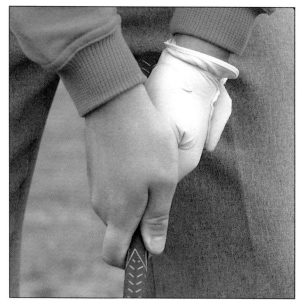

Above: The slicer's grip. The hands are in a weak position as they are turned too far to the left. To correct your grip, move both hands to the right so that the 'V's point more towards your right shoulder than towards your chin. Make sure that you do not grip too tightly.

Opposite: The sequence shows the slice and the swingpath for the slice. Due to a 'weak' grip and poor alignment, the club goes back outside the ball to target line sending the ball to the right. The slicer's swingpath is shown with the club lying on the grass behind the ball indicating the correct target line. The club in the foreground indicates the direction of the swingpath of the slicer, aiming to the left of the ball to target line with the clubface open (right).

Target line

Club swing path

The hook

Definition: The ball begins its flight to the right of your intended target line and then curves severely to the left. The ball tends to fly lower and it lands with topspin, making it a destructive shot because it runs further off-line.

Cause: If you hook the ball the chances are that you hold the club with your left hand too far on top of the grip and your right hand too far under – this is referred to as a *strong* grip. The result being that your clubface returns to the ball in a closed position (aiming left of the target) and creates a swing that becomes too flat on the backswing and too upright on the follow-through. You then start aiming too far right in your set up to compensate and, as stated, this perpetuates and encourages the initial fault.

Due to your strong grip, the face of the club at the top of the backswing will be looking skywards, which is a closed position. This closed position will be reflected at impact and, combined with the swingpath going to the right of the target, imparts anti-clockwise spin on the ball. This shot can be compared to a topspin lob at tennis.

Also, because most right-handed golfers are considerably stronger in their right hand, the tendency is for the strong hand to take over causing the left hand and wrist to collapse.

The cure for hooking is as follows:
- The back of the left hand should face the target, with a maximum of two knuckles visible, when your head is in a central position.
- The right hand should be holding more in the fingers (palm facing target) and with lighter pressure.
- Your feet, knees, hips and shoulders should aim slightly left of your target.
- Check the ball position – it should not be too far back in the stance.
- On the backswing, make your swingpath straighter to achieve a more upright position.
- At the top of the backswing, both wrists should be under the clubshaft (toe of clubface pointing downwards).
- On the downswing, your hips and body should turn to face left of your target.
- Your hands should swing left of your left shoulder at the finish.
- Keep your left hand and wrist firm through impact (back of left hand facing your target).
- The right hand must not overtake and cross over the left too soon.

Equipment: pay attention to the following points:
- The lie of club may be too upright.
- The grip may be too thin.
- The club shaft may be too flexible.

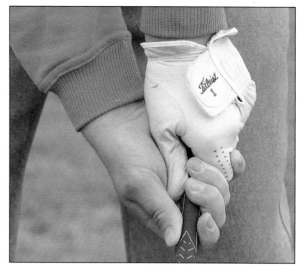

Above: The hooker's grip. The hands use too strong a grip and are turned too far to the right. The left hand is too far on top of the grip and the right hand is too far underneath it. If both 'V's point near to or outside the right shoulder, move them to the left. When you look down at your left hand, you should see two knuckles. If your grip is too strong, you may see three or even more.

Opposite: The sequence shows the hook and the swingpath for the hook. The backswing is too flat, the clubface returns to the ball in a closed position and the follow-through is too upright. The hooker's swingpath is shown, with the club lying on the grass behind the ball indicating the correct target line. The club to the left of the ball shows the direction of the swingpath of the hooker aiming right of the target with the clubface closed (left).

The pull

Definition: The ball flies in a straight line to the left of your intended target. The clubface is square relative to the swingpath, and therefore you are imparting no sidespin on the ball.

Cause: This shot is closely related to the slice as the swingpath is the same, but do not confuse it with a hook purely because the ball has finished left of your target. You may well find that you slice with your long straighter-faced clubs and pull the shorter ones. This is because the lofted clubs impart backspin which reduces the amount of sidespin which is evident with your longer clubs.

To rectify a pulled shot the main factor you must concentrate on is the swingpath which is moving across your body on an out-to-in line.

The cure for pulling is as follows:
● Check your aim (your feet, shoulders and clubface may be aiming left).
● Check the ball position; it must not be too far forward.
● The backswing should be on a more rounded, flatter plane.
● Make a full shoulder turn.
● On the downswing, return on the same path, with your arms close to the right hip.
● On the through-swing, the arms should move away from the left hip.
● Transfer your weight from the right side to the left side on your downswing.
● Adopt a higher finishing position.

Above right: To cure the pull, you must make a more rounded backswing on a flatter plane and a full shoulder turn to keep the club on an inside path. On the downswing, you should return on the same path and transfer your weight to the left foot. Halfway in the downswing, if you have reached the right position, then you have no choice but to hit the ball from the inside.

Right: The swingpath for the pull. The club lying on the grass behind the ball shows the correct target line. The club to the left of the ball shows the swingpath of the pull with the ball finishing left of the target.

The push

Definition: The ball flies in a straight line to the right of your intended target; this is not to be confused with a slice although the ball finishes in a similar place.

Cause: This shot belongs to the same family as the hook, the difference being that your clubface is square relative to the swingpath instead of being closed as in the case of a hooked shot. So you are not imparting any spin on the ball which is simply flying straight in the direction of your swingpath (check the shape of your divot).

Your backswing is a little too much on the inside and your follow-through too upright. Notice the position of your hips in the follow-through – probably you will not have rotated your body around to the left.

The cure for pushing is as follows:
● Check your aim (your feet, shoulders and clubface may be aiming right).
● Check the ball position (it must not be too far back in your stance).
● On the backswing make your swingpath straighter to achieve a more upright position.
● The follow-through should be more rounded with the hips turned, the stomach facing your target or even slightly to the left of it.
● Do not arch your back too much on the follow-through.
● Your hands should swing to the left of your left shoulder at the finish.

Above: The swingpath for the push. The club lying on the grass behind the ball indicates the correct target line. The club to the left of the ball shows the swingpath of the push with the ball finishing to the right of your intended target. The push shot does not curve in flight; it starts to the right of your target and continues to the right. If your set up is acceptable and you still hit a push shot, then you should check your swing. It may be that you are swinging on an in-to-out path with the clubface square to that line.

Skying

Definition: This shot is referred to only when the ball is teed up using a driving club. The flight is very high with little forward momentum, and the ball is struck from the very top part of the clubface, often causing scratch marks to the clubhead.

Cause: You produce this shot when the club approaches the ball from too steep an angle on the downswing and the front edge of the sole of the club hits into the ground. The principal difference between hitting wood shots and iron shots is that irons should be struck on the downswing with a divot after the ball, and woods should be swept away without hitting the ground. Because the shaft of a wood is considerably longer than that of an iron, it will produce a much bigger circle, a wider arc for the clubhead. This makes it possible for the sole of the clubhead to be parallel to the ground at the bottom section of the swing arc, and provided that you position the ball forward in your stance (opposite left instep for the driver) your contact will be at the correct angle to sweep the ball forwards instead of chopping down and producing a skied shot.

The cure for skying is as follows:
● The ball should be positioned forward in your stance.
● Keep your hands level with the back of the ball (sole of club resting flat on the ground).
● Keep the clubhead low to the ground for the start of the backswing (do not break the wrists too early).
● Make your backswing plane flatter (a more rounded shallow arc).
● Transfer your weight onto the right side at the top of the backswing.
● Keep your head behind the ball until after impact.

Opposite: The moment of impact for a normal swing (1 & 2), and for a skied shot (3 & 4). Skying occurs when the downswing is too steep and there is too much clubface below the centre of the ball at impact. Thus, instead of sweeping the ball away on an in-to-out path, the golfer chops down on the ball from too steep an angle, causing it to soar into the sky. By swinging smoothly and rhythmically and keeping the clubhead low to the ground at the start of the backswing and travelling parallel to the ground just before it makes contact with the ball, you can avoid this swing fault.

1

2

3

4

The topped shot

Definition: The ball is struck above its equator by an ascending clubhead, causing a very low shot, a harsh feeling through the clubshaft and often a damaged golf ball. This is also called thinning, which is a semi-top.

Cause: You will suffer with this shot if you try and lift the ball in a scooping action. It is important to realise that golf is different from any other bat or racket game because loft, in varying degrees, is built into the golf clubhead. If you consider a cricket batsman trying to hit a high shot he will have to lean back, with his weight on his back foot, and tip his bat backwards to create a slope that can lift the ball. Also, of course, the cricket ball is in the air, which means that the batsman can attack it from below.

The mechanics are very different when striking a golf ball due to the following factors:
1 The ball is on the ground.
2 The clubhead is lofted.

For your iron shots, particularly the mid to short irons (5 - pw), the golf ball must be struck on the downswing with the clubhead descending and taking a divot after the ball. Many beginners think it wrong to take a divot, fearing that they will jar their arms and damage the course but it is essential to touch the turf at least with the sole of the club if you are to contact the ball squarely in the middle of the clubface. Providing your divot is not too deep and it is after the ball, there is very little resistance from the turf. If you watch any professional playing an iron shot you will always see a divot taken after the ball.

Note: Please remember to replace your divot and push down firmly with your foot each time!

Ensure that your backswing has not become too flat, i.e. swinging your arms around your body on too rounded an arc. In order to be able to swing downwards on to the ball, your clubhead must swing on a straighter line back and up on the backswing. Also a weight transfer from your right side to the left side on the downswing will help you to strike the shot on a downward path.

The cure for topping is as follows:
● Your backswing should be more upright, and not so shallow.
● Pull down with the left arm to start the downswing.
● The hands should be ahead of the clubhead at impact.
● Transfer your weight to a *firm* left side, and turn the hips to face the target.
● Maintain your spine angle (do not stand up).
● Take a divot after the ball.
● Extend your left arm straight at the bottom of the swing arc.

Opposite: Topping occurs when the ball is struck above its equator, causing it to travel along the ground. It is one of the most common swing faults experienced by beginners. Instead of the ball being struck on the downswing with the clubhead descending and taking a divot after the ball, in the topped shot the ball is hit on the upswing by an ascending clubhead, and no divot is taken.

Striking on the toe

Definition: The contact is the toe end of the club striking the inside (nearest to you) half of the ball, causing a shot that veers straight to the right with little power, even though the clubface may well be square. In appearance the shot may be similar to a shank.

Cause: To produce this shot you have changed your swingpath and the clubhead has returned to a point closer to you than at address. Incorrect balance in your set up may well be the cause. Standing too close to the ball will result in you having too much weight on your heels both at address and as you return the ball. However, it is also possible that you are standing too far away making it impossible for your arms to reach the ball, but this is the least likely explanation. You need to be aware of whether you feel that your weight is mainly on your heels or mainly on your toes in order to make your judgement. The correct weight distribution, evenly between your heels and the balls of your feet, is influenced greatly by the distance you stand from the ball. This is one of the great inconsistencies amongst amateur golfers and accounts for erratic shots – due to not standing the same way for every shot.

It is a skill that the good golfer has learned, and so take just a few seconds at your address moving your feet to get settled; do not plant your feet in a solid position and stand motionless before starting your swing. Have a few waggles with the clubhead combined with small foot movements to get finely adjusted.

A very good exercise to help correct toeing is to use two tees to substitute for the ball. One tee should be about a ball's width further from you than the other. Now address the closer tee towards the toe of the club and make a swing that returns to strike both tees. This exercise will then encourage the opposite pattern to emerge, thus returning to a centre clubface contact.

The cure for toeing is as follows:
- Check your balance and distance from the ball.
- Keep the left arm extended through impact.
- Maintain your spine angle (*don't* stand up).
- Swing your arms freely away from your body.
- Your backswing may be too upright.

Left: You can practise this simple exercise to help correct your toeing using two tees instead of a ball. Practise addressing the closer tee towards the toe of the club and then swinging smoothly so that the clubface strikes both tees centrally at impact.

Opposite: Standing too close to the ball in your set up is one of the most common causes of toeing. This causes you to have too much weight on your heels at address. Standing the correct distance from the ball will make you swing on a slightly inclined plane and cause the clubhead to move on an in-to-out swingpath. Perfect your set up so that you stand the same way for every shot and move your feet a little at address to settle them into the right position before you start your swing.

Hitting behind the ball

Definition: The clubhead enters the ground before reaching the ball and therefore a cushion of turf between the clubface and ball causes a severe loss of distance. This is also referred to as 'hitting it fat' or heavy.

Cause: Instinct might tell you that this is the opposite fault to topping but, in fact, the same swing pattern can produce both hitting fat or topping. The reason being that in a similar way the bottom of your swing arc is arriving before the ball; if the ground had not been in the way you would still be striking the ball too much on the upswing, just the same as in a topped shot.

My comments are therefore similar. The concept of 'getting under the ball' is wrong; the loft of the clubface must be allowed to lift the ball. Again, imagine the arc of your swing as a 'U' shape which is on a slant; the bottom of the 'U' must come after the ball.

It is, however, possible to hit behind the ball by having too upright a backswing as well as being too flat, as in the case of topping. If your divot is very deep and behind the ball, the chances are that you have become too upright on the backswing giving a steep angle of attack into the ball. Remember that steep causes deep. The other common fault with this shot is dipping or lowering of height through impact. Ensure that you keep a firm left side at the bottom of your swing.

A good exercise if you suffer from either hitting behind the ball or topping is to place a second golf ball approximately 30cm/12in behind your object ball. This will encourage a downward strike because if you bottom out behind you will contact the wrong ball.

The cure for hitting behind the ball is as follows:
- Pull down and through towards the target with your left arm.
- Maintain the left forearm, wrist and back of hand in line through impact (*don't* scoop).
- Keep the left leg straight supporting your weight, while your hips rotate to face the target.
- If the divot is deep, swing flatter.
- If the divot is shallow, swing more upright.

Above: Hitting behind the ball can be caused by falling back onto the heels and trying to lift the ball at impact while dipping. You can avoid this by keeping your left side firm at the bottom of your swing. Keep the left leg straight to support your weight as you rotate towards the target. Don't scoop the ball but keep your left forearm, wrist and back of hand in line.

Overswing

Definition: This term describes a position at the top of the backswing at which you are out of control and the club shaft will be beyond the horizontal position, although this can vary depending on how supple you are.

Cause: The main cause of overswinging is excessive wrist break and letting go of the club with your left hand at the top of your backswing. Your takeaway should be slow and smooth, and remember that it is only a way of getting into the correct position from which to deliver the downswing. You must not waste energy and lose control by swinging the club back too quickly. In an effort to stop overswinging it is likely that you will fail to turn your shoulders and body fully, which, of course,

Above: The club shaft has gone below the horizontal position. The left arm has bent too much during the backswing and the swing is out of control. Overswinging may also be caused by excessive wrist break.

leads to other problems. The shot pattern resulting from overswing will be varied and inconsistent due to your loss of control.

The cure for overswinging is as follows:
● The left-hand grip must be held firmly in the base of the fingers (excluding the index finger).
● Swing back slowly.
● Use less wrist break, and feel as though your arms and the club shaft swing as one.
● Maintain a firm grip with the top three fingers of the left hand.
● Keep your left arm extended.

Shanking

Definition: The ball is struck from the socket of the clubhead where the face meets the hosel. The ball squirts to the right at a severe angle, usually low. This is a most destructive and confidence shattering shot.

Cause: It is a difficult fault to analyse as there are three ways in which a shank may be produced:

1 Returning with the clubface very open

2 Returning with the clubface very closed.

3 Returning with the clubhead to the ball further from you than at address.

Certainly, if this is a problem for you, one common feature is that your weight moves onto your toes with your knees bent. Make sure that you keep your weight towards your heels during the downswing and follow-through.

If the clubface returns in a very open position then the heel and hosel of the club will arrive at the ball first. On the contrary, a very closed clubface approaching on too rounded an arc can gather the ball into the socket of the club. The easiest way for you to identify your fault is to consider which ball flight you tend to produce normally. If you are inclined to slice, then your shank shot will be of the open clubface variety, and if you hook mainly then it is the closed clubface version.

An occasional shank that afflicts a normally straight hitter is likely to be the third type, caused when the clubhead returns further away

Below: Shanking may be caused by returning with the clubface very closed (left), or by returning with the clubface very open (right) both causing the ball to strike the hosel rather than the clubface.

from you. The divot would still be straight and the clubface square also.

The best remedy is to practise the opposite exercise to the one I suggest for toeing. That is, place two tees approximately a ball's width apart, one further away from you. Now address the furthest one and make a swing that returns to strike only the tee closest to you.

It is a horrible experience to shank but take comfort in the fact that most good players have had a spell of it at some stage or another.

Above: The two tees exercise to cure the shank. Address the tee that is further away from you (top), swing and strike the tee closest to you (above). Practise this regularly and it will help cure this most destructive shot.

Above: The correct position for the clubface and ball at address (top); and the position at impact for the shank (above) when the clubface returns to the ball and strikes it on the hosel, causing it to fly low and to the right.

Guard against these popular faults

Body alignment out

You may well believe that your feet and body should aim at your target. This is incorrect; your clubface should be aimed at the target, whereas your feet, knees, hips and shoulders should be *parallel* to the clubface-to-target line.

Bad posture

An incorrect posture will destroy your swing before it gets started. Teaching pros have a saying: 'Head down will keep us in business forever.' 'I lifted my head' is the reason most amateur golfers give for every bad shot they make. This is simply not true. Remember to keep your *chin up – back straight – bend from your hips*. Yes, keep a steady head but not your head down.

To feel the correct posture, stand erect and hold the clubshaft near the head of the club with your right hand. Place the clubshaft against your back from the base of your spine to the back of your head and then bend forwards from your hips. Be sure to keep the back of your head touching the shaft for as long as possible and only allow it to leave the line sufficiently to look down from the bottom of your eyes to see the ball. A slight knee flex is added and you are now in a position that allows your arms to hang freely downwards from your shoulders and clear of your body.

Right and opposite: Bad posture is one of the most common causes of a poor swing and the development of swing faults. Good posture helps you to control the plane of the swing and aids correct weight distribution and balance. You should not set up with your legs too straight (above right) nor stooping over the ball (right). The correct posture (opposite) is with knees slightly flexed and the weight evenly distributed between both feet. Your hands should not be too low nor too high, so that your arms can swing the club freely and clear of your body. Try to keep your legs feeling subtle, not too stiff nor too straight which leads to shoulder and arm domination at the start of the backswing.

Above: The reverse pivot. The weight has moved to the left side instead of the right side.

Reverse pivot

A correct turn of your body on the backswing should take the majority of your weight onto your right leg, the pivot point being the right hip. If, however, you straighten your right leg and bend your left knee forwards towards a point in front of the ball, this will result in too much weight remaining on your left leg at the top of the backswing. To achieve power and clubhead speed in your swing, you need to have your weight travelling in the direction of the swing. You cannot transfer your weight from the right side to the left, if it is already on your left leg on the backswing. The opposite tends to happen and you will end up falling backwards with a lot of weight on your right foot and a subsequent lack of forward momentum and power.

Swingpath too straight

Although you are attempting to hit the golf ball in a straight line, it is important to realise that the swingpath of the clubhead cannot remain on the straight line beyond roughly the width of your stance and shoulders. If you try and swing back in a straight line too far, it will result in a swaying movement whereby your hips move laterally instead of turning.

The reason that your swing must have a curved element, either side of the centre section, is that you are standing to the side of the golf ball, at differing distances depending on the club you are using. If it were possible to hit a ball positioned between your feet then the line and plane of the swing could be straight and vertical.

Conversely, if the ball was at shoulder height, your swing would have to be travelling on a horizontal arc to return the clubhead to that point. These are the two extremes of plane. When striking a ball that is on the same level as your feet then your arc will need to be working on a plane somewhere between these extremes. As I have explained in earlier fault-finding sequences, your swing arc can be travelling on too flat or too upright a plane for every situation.

Summary

A significant factor in becoming a better golfer is to understand and analyse correctly the cause of a bad shot. You then have a chance of rectifying the problem and not perpetuating it. I must stress here the importance of using a PGA professional to help you trace your faults. We cannot see ourselves, and what we *think* we are doing and the reality are often two very different things. You can use the information in this book in conjunction with your lessons.

But do remember that any changes you make may have to feel uncomfortable initially, otherwise you are not doing anything different. The practice ground is the ideal place to initiate any changes in your game so that you don't take too many thoughts with you on to the course. Correct practice can make perfect, so persevere, enjoy your golf and good luck.

Chapter Eight

Tactics and Strategy

Craig DeFoy

TACTICS AND STRATEGY

We are all familiar with modern professional golf tournaments, whether from being able to attend an event in person or through the wonder of television bringing the top events from around the world into our own homes.

No doubt, the power of Norman and Woosnam, the precision of Faldo and Strange or the sheer inspirational play and finesse of Ballesteros can be awe-inspiring to the average golfer, but surely the superstars play a game that is totally beyond the scope of most of us. Even if this is true, we can still learn from the top players in many ways. The first thing we notice at a tournament is that whilst certain swing fundamentals are common to all the players, they are still instantly recognisable by their own idiosyncrasies and characteristics – each is an individual who does it his own way. All the top players know their own game inside-out and are well aware of their strengths and weaknesses, so that whilst constantly working to improve they have learned to play the game in a way that makes the most of their particular strong points.

Now let's look at your own golf game – are you a long hitter, even if a little wayward? If so, use your power selectively by attacking the par 5s and long 4s and perhaps taking a shorter club off the tee at other times to gain accuracy – there is little point in hitting the ball 250 yards if it finishes in a bush or out of bounds. What about the short hitter? Instead of struggling to hit the ball further, play to your strength by concentrating on being accurate and build your score in this way.

A really good idea is to take a leaf out of the pro's book and plan your way around the course. It would be true to say that after two practice rounds the average tour professional would know a golf course better than the average club player who might have played it most weekends, often for many years. Knowing the yardage from any point on the course is vital to the best players, and so it should be for the lesser golfer too – why use guesswork when it is unnecessary? By all means, pace out your own course from several vantage points on each hole, but this information is not much use if you do not know how far you hit with each club. Find out this information by hitting a number of golf balls and counting your paces to where the *average* shot lands with each club – now you will be far better equipped to tackle the next monthly medal!

Another good idea is to work out your personal par on each hole rather than just going by the card: for instance, if a long par 4 is generally out of reach then why not play it as a par 5 and take the pressure off yourself. Do this for the whole course and see if it doesn't give you a different perspective on your game and make scoring a lot easier.

Finally, learn again from the best players and give up trying to hit those perfect straight shots. Let's face it, they rarely occur so why base your golf game on the unachievable? We all have a tendency to either draw or fade the ball so by all means take this into consideration when you plan a shot. Know your game and play to your strengths!

Opposite: Tour professionals like Ian Woosnam get to know a course on their practice rounds. They pace it out and know the yardages from any point on the course. Even high-handicap golfers would do well to follow their example and to plan their way around a course, especially their own home course. Club selection is equally important, and even if you know the yardage, you must be able to choose the right club to hit the shot in hand as each club has a different loft and will shape the ball differently.

TACTICS AND STRATEGY

Play within your limitations

The number one rule for golfing success at any level is to play the game within your limitations. Although this might sound obvious and simplistic, how often have you found yourself playing a risky or a tricky shot whilst somehow knowing it was 'not on' and probably doomed to failure. Far too frequently when things are going wrong and with the score mounting your instinct will be to go for broke in order to save strokes. More often than not, this will result in a poor shot with your ball in even deeper trouble – hardly surprising since your form is poor and your confidence low.

This is when you should try a little damage limitation and play the safety shot. The time to gamble is when your game is good and things are going well; if the odds are reasonable, take a chance and risk your luck.

The general rule in match-play is to keep the ball in play and force your opponent to have to win a hole on merit, not as a result of a gift from you following an unnecessarily risky or flamboyant shot. There are, however, some occasions when an 'all or nothing' shot is called for and, if successful, it could easily unnerve the opposition and turn the tide of the match. Only employ these tactics as a last resort and remember to trust your swing and commit yourself fully to the shot.

Below: Ian Woosnam is widely acknowledged as a master of golf strategy and tactics.

Warm-up procedures

No self-respecting professional or top amateur player should dream of walking onto the first tee for a competition without warming-up beforehand. This procedure is something all athletes have in common and all would agree to its importance. Since it is seen as vital for highly trained competitors in all sports, then it must be even more crucial for club golfers whose minds and bodies are less attuned to the golf swing and who play the game infrequently.

Having accepted the need for a warm-up, how best to go about it and how long should you or can you spend on this exercise? To loosen those golfing muscles gently and slowly is the most important thing, so don't walk onto the practice range and immediately thrash away with a long club. Rhythm and timing are what we are seeking before a round, so begin as the pros do by gently lobbing a few balls with a pitching wedge. Try to keep the same rhythm and, using no more effort, hit a few balls with a short iron, followed by a mid-iron and so on through the bag until you reach the driver. Even now, concentrate not on distance but on developing a smooth swing so that you step up to that first tee shot not worn out but with your muscles loose and feeling ready to give your best. This session should be seen as a loosening exercise and an opportunity to get yourself into a good rhythm and good frame of mind. Do not look upon it as a time for practice and experiment! Forget any adjustments of technique – this is not the right moment for making changes but for confirming good swing habits.

Let us move now to the putting green for an all important few minutes. If possible, play a few chip shots and then move onto the most important club in your bag – the putter. The crucial elements of good putting are feel and confidence, so resist the temptation to try to hole out from 10 to 20 feet and concentrate instead on acquiring a feel for the coming round. Roll a few balls across the green at no particular target but try to strike each ball in the sweet spot of the putter, and watch it carefully, trying to build up your feel and judgement of the green's pace. Having done that, develop your confidence by

Above: It is important to practise regularly and to concentrate specifically on the weakest areas in your game. Spending twenty minutes hitting a few balls with a range of clubs from short irons through to long irons, and then practising your chipping, pitching and putting, is time well spent, and will loosen you up before a round.

holing a number of putts from a very short distance – get used to the sound and sight of your golf ball dropping into the hole.

This whole session need take no more than around twenty minutes, so next week instead of skidding into the car park and rushing onto the tee totally unprepared, try to make the effort to arrive in good time to loosen up – your golf will almost certainly improve.

Practise the vital areas

Although every shot in golf has an equal value when we count up the score walking off the 18th green, there are certain areas of the game that are more important than others. Before playing a round on most courses we know that we shall be required to play a number of tee shots to par 4s and 5s, whether with a driver or other wood and that a good drive into the fairway will make these holes so much easier. Likewise, regardless of our standard of play, we are all too aware that the wedge is going to be called upon quite frequently for those vital shots from 80 or so yards in. Finally, it is an accepted fact that the average golfer uses his putter for approximately 40 per cent of his total number of shots in an average round.

Obviously, therefore, it is sensible to concentrate most of your practice time on developing your skills and confidence with these scoring clubs. Use them often and learn to make them your allies in the battle against par. If you can hit most of your drives into the fairway and get the ball reasonably close to the pin with your pitch and chip shots, then the rest of your game is under less pressure and is bound to improve as a result. Combine these skills with good putting and your handicap is sure to tumble.

When and how to play safe

When faced with an approach shot to a tightly guarded pin position, you have to work out the percentages of success of each alternative shot you could play. Generally speaking, do not attempt such a stroke with less than a 70 per cent chance of pulling it off.

In the illustration, the penalties of failure in going for the flag are too great and in this and similar situations, play to the larger, safer area of the green and settle for two putts. There are many occasions when we are unable to go for

Opposite: Most courses have a practice tee where you can practise your driving, and a practice green for developing your putting and short game skills. A number of practice drills are outlined later on in this book in Chapter 10.

the green with our second shots – on most par 5s, for instance. The high-handicap golfer instinctively seems to opt for the maximum distance in these situations so as to leave the shortest possible third shot. Most, however, would far prefer to play a full wedge or sand iron into the green rather than a tricky half or three-quarter shot which is generally more difficult and certainly harder on the nerves! Try therefore to lay up into a safe area of fairway offering the best line to the hole and leaving a shot of 80 to 90 yards.

Similarly, on short par 4s; don't reach automatically for your driver. Consider your second shot first and select the club off the tee that is, firstly, giving you a better chance of hitting the fairway, and, secondly, sets up the type of approach that is easiest for you.

When laying up short of a hazard, whether a lake, stream or bunker, don't make the mistake of trying to judge the shot too finely and run the risk of a 'perfect' shot reaching the very trouble you are trying to avoid. Choose a club that you *know* will remain short. Laying up or playing safe is not negative golf; it is simply common sense on occasions, and done properly it will surely reflect in your improved scoring.

Successful putting

Successful putting depends mainly on your ability to hole out consistently from within four feet, so it is essential to get the ball within that radius of the hole. Of the two elements of putting – line and length – by far the more important, certainly on long putts, is length. If you are trying on a long putt to finish within four feet of the hole, then you have that margin on both sides making an eight-foot target. Very few golfers would feel unable to judge the line to that extent, so concentrate instead on feeling the distance to be covered because inconsistent length is the major cause of three-putting. A player who consistently rolls his long putts close to the hole has a powerful weapon in his golfing armoury, and can be the most frustrating of opponents especially in match-play.

Having succeeded in getting your ball within your four-foot range, you now need a reliable method of consistently holing out. The vast majority of short putts that miss do so because of the golfer's anxiety. We expect to hole out from short range, but often the fear of missing causes us to look up too early and try to steer the ball into the hole – the usual result is a poor stroke and a missed putt. Provided that the ball starts on line and is hit positively, it will seldom miss its target since the strength of the putt is almost automatically judged from such short range. Rather than trying to guide the ball into the hole, concentrate instead on rolling it over a point only a few inches along the line. This gives you a task that you can be confident of achieving and therefore quells the anxiety that

is the enemy of the golfer.

Remember that a good putter is a match for anybody, and putting is the great leveller of the game. Putt well during a round and your score is seldom a bad one.

Keep the game simple

This really is the golden rule in competitive play – don't try extra hard hoping for one of your best rounds, and don't be tempted to go for shots that normally you would not expect to pull off. Off the tee, your main priority is to hit the ball onto the fairway – winning golf is seldom played from the rough. If you do go into

the rough or a hazard, make certain of getting back onto the short grass as quickly as possible and avoid the temptation to take risky short-cuts out of desperation. Take your medicine, accept the penalty of dropping a shot and play for a bogey – it is surprising how often you can escape by sinking a long putt.

When hitting your approach shots, unless you are very confident or the situation is desperate, ignore the flag and play for the middle of the green. If successful, you should never be too far from the hole. Remember that sensible golf is winning golf – heroics are best left to the golfing superstars and should only be attempted as a last resort. Take pleasure out of playing to your

Opposite and above: Looking up too early and trying to guide the ball into the hole invariably leads to missed putts. Anxiety and fear of missing are usually to blame.

own game plan and watch how quickly your scores improve.

Some final thoughts

There is an indisputable fact about competitive golf at whatever standard it is played: whenever a player approaches the first tee, he or she is suffering some kind of nervousness. To feel no nerves or apprehension is not only abnormal but counter-productive to good scoring. Even the world's top players who compete at the highest level all the time admit that learning to control these feelings is vital. The most successful golfers are not those who don't feel nervous but those who control this condition best.

Provided that you have warmed-up correctly, your body should be prepared and your rhythm set. Now, before teeing off, if you feel too tight or anxious take a few deep breaths and exhale slowly. This is a simple technique but is widely used and really does work. Finally, and perhaps most importantly, your feelings are not yours alone – take a look at your opponent or playing partner and realise that they are in exactly the same state as you are!

Hopefully you will arrive on the tee having done your golfing homework – you know your own game and have planned the best way for you to play the course. Stick to your gameplan and only deviate from it when the odds are in your favour or your match position becomes really desperate. Play the golf course your own way and let the opposition worry about themselves – no doubt they will have their own problems to contend with!

When playing match-play it is easy to be overcome by your opponent before you even start. Often the better player will be worried about having to give a lot to strokes and will be struck by the thought that although he might be a superior golfer, he now has to prove it and, let's face it, nobody likes to lose to a worse player. The higher handicapper, on the other hand, is all too aware of his shortcomings and feels that only his best or even better will do. By trying to play beyond himself and not look too bad, he will only succeed in sabotaging his own chances of success.

Likewise, the long hitter – usually a little wayward – is affected by the shorter but more accurate one, whilst he is frequently tempted into making mistakes by trying to keep up off the tee. The answer to all of these problems is simple – play your own game and turn every situation to your own advantage. Put yourself into your opponent's shoes and ask yourself what he might be feeling about you. The reply can often prove to be just the encouragement you need.

Similarly, if the course is not to your liking or the weather not good, console yourself with the understanding that the same course and weather conditions really do apply to everybody else, so the player who just gets on with the job at hand is the one most likely to succeed.

We are all aware that our play on a given hole is greatly affected by our experience of the round this far. Trying to play a hole well when feeling either depressed or over-excited is not being fair on ourselves. How then do we avoid this pressure? After all, it is only human to be annoyed and frustrated if our game is going badly. Equally, it is only normal for the adrenaline to be pumping through our veins if we have a particularly good score going. Contrast your feelings therefore with those you had on the first tee when you were full of hope and expectation but had no experience of success or failure to call upon. Try to play every hole as if it was the first one – by all means, enjoy your good shots and even allow some frustration at the bad ones, but try to put these thoughts out of your head and play the next hole as number one!

It has often been said that golf is a funny game. True, we really don't know what might happen next. The history of the game is littered with incredible shots and remarkable comebacks, so whatever your situation, keep trying till the round is over. As long as you are able to say at the 19th hole that you gave of your best, then you can ask no more of yourself.

Just one final thought – golf is a game and we are all fortunate enough to be able to play it, at whatever standard. Never forget that it really is only meant to be fun after all.

Chapter Nine
Mind Over Body

Craig DeFoy

Millions of words have been written in thousands of books dedicated to improving the swing and scoring ability of the average golfer. Only in recent years, however, have golfers been awakened to the role of the mind in the game.

Unlike most ball games, golf does not involve a moving ball, and no time limit is placed upon the execution of a shot. This means that golf is not a 'reaction' game unlike, say, football, tennis or cricket which demand a lot of movement of the player and leave little time to think 'how' to perform the kick, stroke, catch or whatever. Furthermore, golf is an individual game for the most part with every stroke counting and having an equal value – no second service in this game! Yet again, golf is not played on a pitch or court of specific size, nor is it played in regular conditions. Unlike other games, the weather, for instance, has to be really extreme for a golf competition to be abandoned or even postponed. No moving ball to react to then – just a small, round, white object sitting there waiting for you to hit it to a distant target using a long club with a very small hitting surface!

All of these factors combine to make golf not only a tremendous challenge, but surely the ultimate sporting test of your body and, even more importantly, the mind. Simply hitting a golf ball reasonably well with any consistency is difficult enough, but manoeuvring it round the course with all the variables of distance, lie, weather conditions etc., and with no second chances, is a very demanding task both physically and mentally!

We humans have a unique capacity to allow both external and internal stimuli to interfere with our ability to perform a physical task that we know ourselves to be capable of carrying out successfully. If you doubt how the mind can influence your performance, consider the following scenario.

You are faced with a shot on the practice range with your favourite five iron – no problem, your confidence is high and you expect to be successful. Should you not therefore be equally confident when faced with the same shot only this time standing on the final fairway and needing to hit the green to break your handicap or, even worse, to win the Club Championship? Perhaps so in theory, but we all know that the different circumstances have created all kinds of thoughts in your mind adding up to a word we all hear so often – pressure.

During the next few pages we shall examine the phenomenon further and look for ways of coping with it more successfully – after all, the winners seem to be able to do so.

Fear of failure

Something we are often loathe to admit to is a fear of failure. Everything in our upbringing and schooling promotes in us a desire to succeed. Success is what we are taught to strive for in all walks of life, and yet we simply *cannot* be successful *all* the time. Logic and experience tell us that we are bound to fail sometimes, and yet we hate to face up to this fact.

If failure is a life-threatening fact then we are entitled to feel under pressure – consider the well-known plank walking example. We are able to stroll along a plank on the ground with no concern, yet placing the same plank 30m/100ft up in the air would cause most of us to crawl along it!

Contrast this then with our fear of missing a short putt or driving the ball down a narrow fairway bordered by an out-of-bounds fence. Should the ball miss the hole or finish on the wrong side of the fence, would it really affect the quality of our lives that much? The answer obviously is no – at worst, our score is affected and our pride is perhaps hurt for a moment or two. We might feel foolish but we surely cannot expect to be perfect, can we?

Facing up to the *real* consequences of failing on any particular stroke therefore will help you to release and give it your best swing – after all, when all is said and done what else can you do?

Trying too hard

'If at first you don't succeed, try, try again.' This saying is well-known to all of us – we are all part of a culture that praises effort above all else. Many parents will say to their children things like, 'If you try hard enough, you will succeed in the end' or 'As long as you try your hardest, then we will be proud of you'.

These are admirable sentiments but what is trying? We tend to equate trying hard with a furrowed brow and a look of grim determination, but is this approach really successful? Try the following simple experiment.

Have someone throw a golf ball into your hand from a short distance away – note how accurate he is while relaxed. Now ask him to perform the same simple task but suggest that it is really *vital* that he throws the ball into your hand. Watch the change of expression on his face and then see whether he is more or less accurate. Invariably, he will be more successful at first but, of course, he was trying then too – he was just unaware of it and not questioning his ability.

The same applies to golf – simply allowing your swing to perform rather than making yourself try harder is always more successful. A good illustration of this is your attitude on the 18th tee when heading for a good, or possibly winning, score. You tell yourself to concentrate, swing slowly, keep your head still, just one more good shot and I'm home – and what happens? More often than not you hit a bad shot through trying too hard and blow your winning chances.

Alternatively, a top player in the same position is telling himself to relax and trust his swing – the product after all of long hours of practice – and after deciding on a particular type of shot, just allow his ability to express itself.

Regardless of your ability or standard of play, you will find that this approach will help you to not only play better, but to enjoy your game more, too.

Overtightness

As we have seen, fear of failure and over-trying can cause major problems for the golfer, but how do these things manifest themselves in the golf swing? Inevitably, what happens is that your muscles become too tight causing your swing to become shorter and jerkier with a distinct lack of smoothness and rhythm. Watch a fellow competitor and compare his practice swing with the one used under pressure.

Unfortunately, what applies to him also applies to you – it's just that we are seldom aware of the way we look ourselves.

If your swing is tight, then you will suffer from a tendency to steer the ball and being unable to release the clubhead properly severely reduces clubhead speed which is reflected in a dramatic loss of power and distance.

How can we learn to cope with this problem? There are many techniques that help an athlete to combat tension and overtightness including controlled breathing, but identifying exactly where the tightness occurs within the swing allows us to set about curing the problem. Begin by checking on your grip of the club – is it firm enough to control the clubhead and yet create a feeling of freedom and power, or are you hanging on for dear life as if clinging to a live snake? If your grip is too tight, note how tension occurs in your wrists and forearms. This is then transmitted to your shoulders and so on, with disastrous results. Having corrected the strength of your hold on the club, now allow your other muscles to be relaxed and yet ready for action.

Whilst hitting the golf ball, make sure that you *swing* the clubhead *through* the ball. Try this key thought and you should begin to notice quite a difference in your results.

Visualization

Jack Nicklaus has said that he never allows himself to hit a shot before forming a very clear mental picture of what he is attempting. This process, which we call visualization, is common to all good players but is seldom used by the average golfer.

To stand a good chance of success, a golf shot has to be carefully planned before being executed. Try standing over your shot and picture firstly the ball sitting on the green where you would like it to finish, and then imagine its flight path from the centre of your clubface to the target. Once you have this image strongly in place simply move into your pre-shot routine and swing.

You will find that this organised approach to your shots will be far more beneficial than a haphazard 'hit and hope' routine.

Above: Jack Nicklaus never hits a ball without visualizing first the shot he wants to play. Like him, you should be positive and carefully plan a shot that is within your capabilities. Don't be negative and imagine slicing the ball, or you will probably end up doing so.

Play golf not swing

It has always seemed to me that there are two games of golf – the golf club swinging game and the game of golf itself. The practice range is the place where you should be working on your technique and trying to improve your ball striking skill. Unfortunately, it is all too easy to over-complicate the technical side of the game and many people become so absorbed in what the various parts of their bodies are doing that they think only in this one dimension.

The variables of golf are so great that it is impossible to concentrate on scoring whilst concerning yourself with 'how to swing'.

Practising on technique is essential if improvement is to be made, but once you step onto the first tee your attention should be focused on manoeuvring the ball around the course in the fewest possible strokes. Take into account all the various factors that influence your club and shot selection and then remember to place your faith in all those hours spent on the practice range and trust your natural swing. This approach will allow you to enjoy the challenge of playing the game of golf in a more positive frame of mind.

Enjoy your success

Whilst we are aware that golf can prove to be a hugely frustrating exercise we should all remember that it is after all just a game. For the professional, of course, it is a business but when the pro stops enjoying the game for its own sake he quickly finds his earning potential decreasing. Nothing is more frustrating for the teacher than the pupil who takes golf too seriously. When we lose our sense of enjoyment, we are unable to concentrate properly and therefore cannot continue to learn.

A sense of humour is essential in trying to play a game that is so demanding and which, because of its difficulty, dictates that we frequently fail in our attempts to hit those elusive perfect shots. Examine your own approach – do you drive home after a weekend game cursing the errors you made, or do you think more of the one or two really good shots that made your day such a pleasure?

If your attitude is perhaps too grim, give yourself a break – you do play the game from choice after all. Keep your mental attitude positive but be realistic – nobody succeeds all the time. Try not to over-analyse the reasons for your poor shots but concentrate instead on the good ones.

Don't be afraid to congratulate yourself on your successes and allow yourself a little inward smile – after all, it is only a game!

Chapter Ten

The Importance of Practice

Robin Mann

This chapter is devoted to practice and how it can help you to improve your game. The fundamental principle of golf is to create the perfect impact. This is done via the set up and swing as dealt with earlier in the book. To create perfect impact on a regular basis, you must develop a technically sound and repeating set up and swing. This can be done only by practice. By regularly grooving your set up and swing, you will improve dramatically your chances of reproducing them on the golf course.

For novice players and tournament professionals alike, practice also provides a wonderful opportunity to explore the full range of shots in golf. Some of these may never be required, but experimentation on the practice ground is essential in order to understand your own swing. Thought patterns can be developed which can be used on the course to produce a particular type of shot. This said, it is always a good idea to have a particular goal in mind during each practice session, as practice without purpose can prove wasteful. When the greatest players in the world produce marvellous shots, they are merely executing out on the course in tournament conditions what has taken many painstaking hours to achieve in practice. A good example of this is when the legendary Ben Hogan was in contention for the US Open of 1950. He produced a remarkable two iron shot at the final hole to tie for first place, and subsequently won the play-off the following day. He attached more importance to that two iron shot, but he discovered that his view of it was very different from that held by his friends, spectators and the media. They were inclined to think that it was an inspired shot in a pressured situation, but Hogan maintained that he had been practising that shot since he was twelve years old and through practice was able to execute the shot in a required situation. Certainly in modern times, the improvement of standards in golf owes as much to the tremendous dedication of the players as it does to the new technology of clubs and balls. It is not uncommon to hear of professionals practising for four or five hours a day as they strive to polish their swings, and improve their putting and bunker play in preparation for tournaments.

Hopefully, you will now begin to realise that practice is as important in golf as it is in any other sport. No matter what standard of player you are, practice will enable you to improve your game and thereby gain further enjoyment from it. Good practice will never go unrewarded and improvements may be seen very rapidly. However, you must practise the right technique and procedures – hours spent repeating the wrong grip or an incorrect set up are hours wasted, and no benefit will be gained. Thus it is important to enlist the help of a qualified professional in the early stages of learning so that the right movements are ingrained. Sometimes it is a good idea to practise in pairs, as your partner may be able to spot a fault or weakness in your game of which you are are not aware. Help with alignment is very important, and a partner standing behind you as you .address the ball is ideally placed to check that you are lined up correctly.

Physical and mental benefits of practice

Practice also imposes a certain mental and physical discipline, which builds confidence in the long run. Grooving a sound, repeating swing depends on muscle memory, i.e. the ability of a muscle to repeat a given task. Through many practice swings, muscles automatically remember how they are supposed to interact, and in the tension of a competition or a monthly medal this can be vital. Comfort can be gained from the knowledge that the swing will not break down because the muscles know how to function. Repeated use of these muscles also helps to build and strengthen them. This will result in a more energy-efficient swing that is less tiring and feels easy to perform.

Practice also helps to boost confidence, which, in turn, eases the mental challenge of golf. Knowing that you have hit a particular shot many times on the practice ground will increase your belief that you can play that shot during the course of a game. This can be very important when confronted with, say, a shot over water or where a hole demands for the ball to be moved from right to left in the air. It was once said that golf is played in the smallest area of any sport: the few inches between your ears. As so much depends on the mental side of golf, it makes sense to increase your self-belief by practising a variety of shots regularly.

Practising off the course

Much good work can be done without even touching a golf ball. A few minutes a day spent taking your grip can help tremendously. Whether you are a novice still trying to come to terms with the intricacies of the grip, or an established golfer who feels that he has mastered this part of the game, this drill is good for developing the muscles in the hands and you can never spend too much time on this vital area. Another very useful drill is 'dry-swinging' without a club. This again teaches and trains the muscles involved in the swing and is a good rehearsal before the act of actually hitting the ball. A few dry swings taken before each shot during a round of golf can sometimes help. This will ensure that you have made a final decision about the exact shot you intend to play, and you may find it useful to visualize the shot as you dry swing. You may feel almost as though you have already played the shot as you stand to address the ball and will not be too surprised if the ball flies off on its intended path. With a clearer image of what you want to do in mind, the correct execution of the shot is more likely to follow.

Establishing a practice routine

It is a good idea to develop your own routine for practice sessions *and* shots on the golf course. A set routine is more likely to be repeated than a haphazard one and this, in turn, will improve the consistency of both your set up and swing. You may wish to add to the suggestions below or even ignore them and use your own. But however you proceed, an organised session will bring dividends and could help you to knock vital points off your score.

The most benefit can be gained from practice on a regular basis. Obviously it may not be practical or possible for you to spend an hour or

Dry-swing exercise

Dry swinging without a club helps train the muscles used in the golf swing. You can also practise dry swinging before you hit a shot on the course, and try to visualize the shot you wish to make while doing so. You will then be better equipped to play the shot, armed with a clearer idea of where you want the ball to fly, and the ball is more likely to be on target.

more a day in this manner, but the more often you are able to practise, the faster you will find that you improve.

Before starting the session, you should have a clear objective. With a particular aim in mind, practice can prove far more worthwhile. As well as helping to maintain your level of concentration, a sense of achievement can be felt if you achieve your goal. This objective may be something as simple as checking ball position in the stance, or moving the ball from right to left to help on a particular hole on your local course. With your goal in mind, you are now ready to move to the practice ground. The following routine is designed to help you practise effectively. Try it out for yourself and amend it as you think fit to accommodate your individual needs.

1 Pre-session warm-up

Before hitting any golf balls, it is wise to spend a few minutes stretching the muscles that are about to be called into action. This will help to prevent injury and make the swing feel smoother and easier. If you find that you have little or no time to hit some balls before a round or competition, some warm-up stretching before stepping on to the first tee can prove invaluable. You may find your rhythm sooner and shots could be saved that normally go astray early in the round.

A few dry swings at half speed should be the next drill to perform. With just a 9 iron in your hands, gently wind and un-wind, just brushing the grass lightly on the throughswing. You can gradually increase the tempo of the practice swing until it reaches normal speed.

2 Starting to strike balls

You should by now feel ready to start hitting balls. A sensible progression is to begin with just a pitching wedge or sand iron and work slowly up through the irons. About 50 per cent effort is sufficient at first to develop a feeling for the ball. After 10 or 15 shots with each club, move up to the next iron. When you feel ready, hit about 10 full drives. To finish with, hit some gentle pitch-

The feet together exercise

1

The main purpose of this exercise is to develop balance and shoulder turn. All great players have great balance and, with this exercise, you too can develop balance and turn. When practising or even outside in your garden, take a 5, 6 or 7 iron or a driver and simply place your heels, toes and knees together with your knees slightly flexed, the object being to keep the lower body (waist down) as still as possible when you swing. Then gently try to turn only

2

3

your shoulders. A good thought pattern is to let the left shoulder go down and under your chin whilst keeping the legs fairly still. When you first do this, the swing will feel short, but don't worry. The muscles, if gently reminded, will gradually stretch and your shoulder turn will increase. The balance developed whilst the feet are together will become very apparent once you take your normal stance again.

With the advent of the 1990s many top-flight professionals are working on keeping their lower body still and more of an anchor to the ground, while the upper body just winds and unwinds. One great side effect of this exercise is tempo, and a smooth golf swing. It is very difficult to swing quickly with your feet together as you will find. You may at first need to take a step to regain your balance if the swing is too fast.

ing wedges. This will serve to slow down your tempo, which may have increased after some full-blooded swings. This way, you will have covered the full range of clubs in your bag.

3 Working on your goal

By now you should be fully warmed up and ready to tackle the objective you have in mind. Unless you have a particular club in mind, a seven iron is recommended for the practice session. Work steadily until you feel that you have achieved what you set out to do.

4 Varying your practice

It is sensible to break up your practice session if you feel yourself entering a rut. Although practice should be with purpose, it should also be enjoyable to get the most out of the game. Varying the type of shots you attempt to hit will also enable you to try out new ideas. Try moving a few shots from right to left and then some the other way. Hit some shots high over an imaginary tree and others low as if into a headwind. It will also help if you try to visualize targets or particular hazards to be avoided such as trees on the right or a pond on the left. By developing a full range of shots on the practice ground, you will find yourself far better equipped to deal with a difficult situation on the course. Imagining targets is of far more use than just hitting shots aimlessly into an empty field. How many players have been heard to say, 'I can play so well in practice, so why can't I put it together on the course?' This can be attributed largely to the fact that they either practise without objectives, or they see a hazard on the course that was not there on the practice ground and go to pieces. By picturing these hazards on the range and practising the shots to cope with them, you are giving yourself a much improved chance of scoring well on the course.

5 Short game and putting

To wind a session down, conclude with some shots out of a bunker and around the green.

The slow motion exercise

When you practise, it is so easy to just stand around and hit hundreds of golf balls and not learn anything, sometimes even getting worse and ingraining faults. The Slow Motion Exercise is a great way for you to learn about whatever you are working on in your swing, be it legs, shoulders, balance etc.

To do the exercise, simply try to slow the swing down to take 10-15 seconds. From your set up, slowly and smoothly take the club back, feeling that you are making a good shoulder turn, with firm legs and good balance. The second half of your backswing will be tough, so do it gradually. From the top of the backswing learn to get the clubhead returning square at impact, and ensure that the club goes through and down the target-line and then to a full finish position. Top professionals use this exercise because, like you, they will be able to feel what is happening in their swing.

The spiral putting practice routine

Place about 24 balls in a spiral around a selected hole on the putting green, the closest ball being three feet from the hole, and vary the distance until the last is 20-35 feet from the hole. Try to read the line of each putt and also to get the pace of the putt correct, starting at 3 feet and working outwards. The advantage of this routine is that you learn to read greens and develop a feel for the pace. When this becomes easier, start to mix up the distances – for example, 15 feet, then 4 feet, 7 feet, 20 feet and 10 feet. This is especially good because this is the way the footage of putts comes to you on each green on the course.

The chipping routine

Take a number of practice balls to about 10 feet off the edge of the putting green. The purpose of this exercise is to learn that all of your iron clubs have a use around the putting green. Firstly take your sand iron and chip two or three balls on to the edge of the putting green. Watch the amount of roll on the shot after the ball has hit the green, then move through the clubs: wedge, 9 iron, 8, 7, 6, 5, 4 and 3 irons. You will notice that the lower the number of the club, the more the roll out on the shot.

Place a marker three feet onto the green where you want all your chip shots to pitch. Once you have hit some shots with each club, pick out four different hole positions and learn which club in your bag is the right one to pitch three feet on the green and roll out to the flag. To get an idea of the range of the clubs, use this example:

Wedge	*50% in the air*	*50% roll*
7 Iron	*33% in the air*	*66% roll*
4 Iron	*20% in the air*	*80% roll*

As in the putting exercise, this is especially good for developing feel.

With a sand wedge in the bunker, start by making a mark in the sand where the ball would be. Then without the ball, take your set up and practise a few shots to get the feeling of the club sliding into the sand and then out again. Many players are afraid when confronted with a bunker shot but, again, with the help of practice you can see that this fear is ill-founded. Move on and play some shots out of varying lies and of varying distance. Practise off uphill and downhill lies, out of plugged lies and good lies.

After this hit some shots of varying length around the green. Try to develop the habit of only taking two shots from just off the green. This is an area where many shots go to waste during a round, so you should attach as much importance to this part of the game as to the long game. With regular practice, you can build up your confidence in this area.

Some practice putting can then round off the session. Try to hit as many different putts of different lengths as possible in order to develop 'feel'. Putting to a tee peg stuck into the ground rather than at a hole can be useful because this removes any frustration about missing putts.

Summary

I have just outlined a full practice session; one that you may not always have the time to follow. However, if you can just start with a gradual warm-up and then manage to hit a full range of shots, your time spent practising will soon be rewarded on the course. As one final thought on practice, bear this in mind: Gary Player was once accused of being lucky by a spectator after holing what at first appeared to be a difficult shot. He replied, 'Yes, but it's funny because the more I practise, the luckier I get!'

Acknowledgements

The publishers would like to thank the following individuals and organisations for their help in compiling this book:

Allsport, Phil Inglis, Mark Shearman and Stillview Photography for supplying the photographs.

Lawrence Farmer, Robin Mann, Paul Wilby and Ricky Willison for appearing in the photographs.

Finn Valley Golf Centre and West Middlesex Golf Club for permitting us to photograph the instructional pictures and sequences on their courses.